W9-BFZ-077

Praise for *Freewheeling Through Ireland*

'He tells us: "I found that the entire Republic was in a grand conspiracy to make sure I enjoyed myself" – and Enfield's stories will make you weep with laughter'

The Oldie

'Enfield's writing is gently amusing and he is good on the quainter details of life in Ireland, particularly rural life. This is a sometimes witty and often well-observed account of some of the most beautiful and magical spots in the rugged Irish landscape and the fishermen, landladies, publicans and horse-dealers who people it'

Sunday Telegraph

'With a wit that's dryer than a martini and an unfailing sense of the absurd, Mr Enfield is the perfect companion with which to travel… a book that is liberally sprinkled with literary tips and historical references… If you are planning a trip, don't leave it behind and if you are not, this might just tempt you'

Saga *Travellers News*

Praise for *Greece On My Wheels*

'Enfield not only impresses – he informs and delights...
the overall effect is charming... This is a man with a deep
affection for the beauty and culture of the land he is gliding
through'

Wanderlust magazine

'I would not have expected an account of one man's travels
around Greece on a bicycle to be such fun... This is so much
more than a travelogue... It is a delightful introduction to a
wonderful country, and a story well told'

Saga _Travellers News_

'The most charming travelogue I've read this year. Mr
Enfield takes the reader on a cycling tour, a history lesson
and a literary safari that combines old world wit and charm
with a sweeping breadth of knowledge. This volume should
be on every creative writing course syllabus as an example of
travel writing at its best'

**Paul Blezard, presenter and producer
of *Between the Lines* and *Footnotes***

Praise for *Downhill All the Way*

'With all the excitement of the Tour de France, Edward Enfield's *Downhill All the Way* provides welcome respite for those of us less inclined to mountains. Retiree Enfield recounts his north-south crossing of France in a humorous, heart-warming fashion. The charming anecdotes and his invaluable Continental touring tips combine to make this ideal summer reading'

London Cyclist

'A charming and witty work!'

Destination France

'In a journey fraught with incident – including being banned from a swimming pool on account of his trunks being too decent – Edward's skills as a narrator combined with his gentle humour and sharp observer's eye result in yet another delightful travel book from the pedal-powered pensioner. Through the Rhône and down to Provence and the Camargue, Edward is witty and informative as always. There's also a funny introduction to the book written by Harry Enfield, Edward's very talented comedian son'

Provence Life

DAWDLING BY THE DANUBE

Summersdale Publishers Ltd
46 West Street
Chichester
West Sussex
PO19 1RP
UK

www.summersdale.com

Printed and bound in Great Britain

ISBN: 1-84024-637-5
ISBN 13: 978-1-84024-637-7

DAWDLING
BY THE DANUBE
With Journeys in Bavaria and Poland

EDWARD ENFIELD

summersdale

Coral Nina Katie Rosalind Christina Archie Poppy Kitty Lucas Nell

To my ten grandchildren

ABOUT THE AUTHOR

Edward Enfield's chief characteristic is, he says, that he is very old. He is old enough to have been evacuated to Canada during the war, and old enough to have spent many hours at school and Oxford struggling to write Greek and Latin verses (which practice is now obsolete). He is sufficiently old to have done National Service in Germany and to have worked for Cathay Pacific Airways when they only had three aeroplanes.

When he retired from his eventual employment in local government, he was given, by Richard Ingrams, a suitable niche in the form of a regular column in *The Oldie* magazine, and he has written for many other publications including the *Express*, *Evening Standard*, *Telegraph*, *Guardian*, *Sunday Telegraph* and *Radio Times*. His elderly voice was often heard on radio, as co-presenter of *Double Vision* and as presenter of *Free Spirits*, the last of the *Down Your Way* series and *Enfield Pedals After Byron*. He has been a senior presence on television in, for example, *Watchdog* and the BBC's *Holiday* programme, *Points of View* and *The Heaven and Earth Show*.

He has one wife, four children and ten grandchildren.

CONTENTS

INTRODUCTION

When it comes to introductions, the world divides into those who read them and those who don't, with those who don't probably outnumbering those that do by about nine to one. I am generally one of those who does not, as I am usually keen to get on with the book itself without bothering about what comes before. Sometimes, though, I read the introduction after I have finished the book, which is the best way if it happens to be a classical novel, as these have introductions written by editors who discuss the plot so fully that they completely give the game away. I recently made the mistake of reading the introduction to a Henry James novel before I started the book, and as a result I knew exactly who was going to marry whom, when I ought to have been kept in suspense.

In the hope that some of those who read this book will sooner or later get round to the introduction, I will say that its purpose is to thank two people for the help they gave me in writing it. The first is Jennifer Barclay of Summersdale Publishers, who sent me back the drafts of each section with her most helpful and incisive comments. She has also invented what I think is a completely new editorial tool in the form of a smiley face. It looks like this:

and she puts it in the margin of any passage which makes her smile or laugh. As I am quite incapable of judging my own work and each time wondered if she would damn each section out of hand and demand the return of my advance, it was always enormously encouraging to find a sprinkling of smiley faces to indicate those parts that had met with her approval. I have also to thank Bill Billington, a friend and colleague over many years and a German scholar good enough to have spent the war cracking codes at Bletchley Park. He put me right on several points of German, cast his eye over the Romantic Road and Danube sections, and drew my attention to two omissions which I have since rectified.

In gratitude to those who have read thus far I will pass on a tip which I got from George Byam-Shaw, a friend from Oxford days. I sent him a copy of my book about Greece and he replied by return of post, saying, 'I make it a rule always to thank an author for his book before reading it – it saves possible embarrassment.' You can do this with any book given to you by anyone, not necessarily the author. If you have been made a present of, say, 'A Life of J. R. R. Tolkien', and don't like the look of it, write at once to say how delighted you are to have it, how much you look forward to reading it, put it on a shelf and after a decent interval take it to the Oxfam shop. You may of course treat *Dawdling By the Danube* in exactly this way if it has been forced upon you by some well-meaning friend.

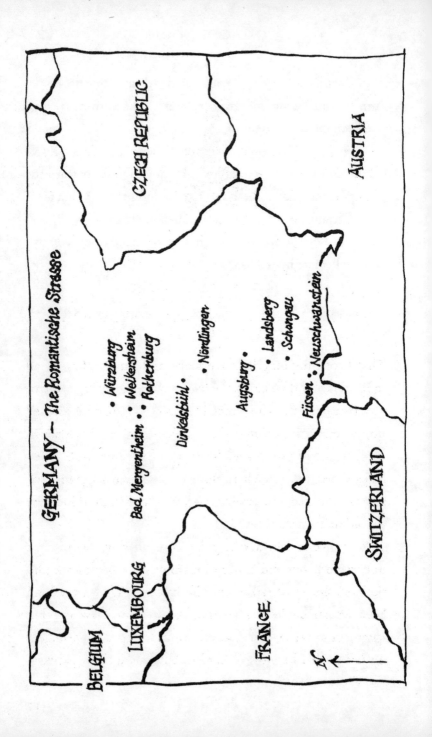

THE ROMANTIC ROAD – 1997
WITH DIGRESSIONS AND DEVIATIONS

That I rode my bicycle in Germany and Austria, first of all in Bavaria and then along the banks of the Danube, is due to a German couple who I met in Greece. We had all pitched up, on our bicycles, in a pleasant hotel called the Alsos in an unattractive town called Skala, on the Peloponnese. They had spotted me somewhere along the route earlier in the day, and as I entered a taverna that evening they waved me over to join them at their table.

We conversed in a triangular sort of way, because he understood, but did not speak, English, whereas she did both, so she and I talked, and he listened. They were both keen cyclists and he was, I gathered, a successful lawyer who, having more sense than most successful lawyers, had arranged his life so that he worked hard in bursts and then, between bursts, abandoned the law and went cycling with his wife. When we had exhausted Greece as a topic of conversation – where we had been, what we had seen, where we were going, then, 'What is it like cycling in Germany?' I asked.

'Very good,' said she.

'Give me some routes,' said I, 'but be careful because whatever you tell me to do I shall probably do it, so take it seriously.'

So with a pen from my pocket and table napkins from the taverna she wrote out two routes. On one napkin she wrote:

Romantic Road: (Neuschwanstein)
Füssen/Allgäu
Schongau
Landsberg
Augsburg
Nördlingen
Dinkelsbühl
Rothenburg
Würzburg

On the other napkin she wrote:

Passau (Germ)
Wien (Austria)
Only Bike-Streets on the Donau

I think, but I am not certain, that she said that of the two the Romantic Road is the stiffer, and the ride by the Danube from Passau to Vienna the less taxing.

It was, I now realize, quite a feat of memory to have rattled off the towns and cities of the Romantic Road, otherwise Romantische Strasse, all in the right order from south to north. It is not something I could repeat, though I have done the ride. I was perfectly in earnest in asking her to take my question seriously, as I had been thinking, in an idle sort of way, of going to Germany with my bicycle, and it only needed a chance encounter such as this to nudge me into doing it. That and a further chance remark, which I will come to in a moment, did the trick.

I had thought for some time that there must be something funny about Germany because, except for hard-drinking types at the Munich beer festival, I never heard of anybody going there for a holiday. Every year after Christmas the newspapers were full of advertisements for Greek islands, French cottages, Spanish apartments, Tuscan villas and Turkish boats with funny names, but on the subject of Germany they were silent. When I was still working in local government the people in my office used to do strange things such as harness caravans to the backs of their cars and drag them all the way to Portugal, and then, two weeks later, drag them all the way back. My neighbour, Ted Barclay, went to Turkey on one of the funny boats, and when he came back he said, in his refreshing way:

'Turkey is quite unspoiled and I am not going back again until they have spoiled it, because as it is now, it is horrible.' Not one of all these people, as far as I know, ever went to Germany. This was, in my view, the first of two advantages, because if I went to Germany there should be no other English tourists.

There are travellers who, when abroad, are delighted to see a fellow countryman. They strike up acquaintanceships which ripen into short friendships; they exchange addresses, part with regret, send each other Christmas cards for a couple of years, and then forget each other. Not I. There are quite enough Englishmen at home without my wanting to run into them abroad. Thinking of this now reminds me of the time that I went with my wife and children to Rhodes. I was still working in the Education Department of West Sussex County Council, and at that time the name of the director of education was G. R. Potter. I was coming out of the sea at Lindos when a man whom I did not recognize came up, said he was the newly appointed West Sussex county surveyor, and wasn't Lindos a fine place? Once he was safely out of earshot I said to my wife: 'This is terrible. We come all the way to Lindos to get away from home, and what happens? Local government officers start popping up all over the place. The next thing we know, G. R. Potter will emerge from behind a rock.'

At this, a tall man who was lying full-length on the sand with his hat over his face gave out a hollow and melancholy groan and said, in the most feeling tones imaginable, 'God forbid!'

Who he was, why he had a particular aversion to the now-deceased G. R. Potter – these are mysteries. He did not remove his hat from his face or make any further observations, but I felt that he and I were somehow fellow spirits, with a common wish to avoid each other.

So, if I went to Germany there ought to be no Englishmen, which was the first advantage. Furthermore, if I went in August there would probably be no Germans, or at least not many, as most of them would be in Greece, France, Spain, Italy or Turkey. Everyone I spoke to, including those who dragged their caravans to Portugal, said that there were Germans everywhere, performing a sort of ritual in seizing the best places by the swimming pool. That they do this, and that it is not a matter of myth, I can confirm. One January my wife and I went to Madeira and stayed in a lovely hotel with an open-air swimming pool. The sun shone so determinedly that even in January it was very pleasant to swim in the pool, and round it there were chairs enough for all, but nevertheless the resident Germans came out early and, from sheer force of habit, marked some of them out for their exclusive use by draping towels on them before they went in to breakfast. Well, if they were doing that all over the rest of Europe all through the summer, Germany itself in August could hardly be crowded. To me, therefore, who has a taste for solitude, the prospect of a Germany free of Englishmen and largely empty of the native population was an attractive one.

I should say that I had, in my youth, spent eighteen months in Germany as a National Service officer in the 8th Hussars, stationed in Lüneburg. It was in a way, a cloistered existence. The only Germans we spoke to were the mess waiters, the grooms who looked after our horses, and a count who had lost his estates to the Russians in East Prussia, and was reduced to earning a living by teaching us to ride. Otherwise we spoke only to fellow soldiers and their wives. We went to Hanover, but only to the races. I spent one evening in Hamburg, where a fellow subaltern and I walked nervously down the Reepebahn, a street with plate-glass windows in which lightly-clad women sat and beckoned to us to come inside. We were much too timid to accept their invitations, and were secretly glad when we got to the far end without feeling the heavy hand of a military policeman on the shoulder of one or other of us, as the Reepebahn was officially off limits to the military. Some Other Ranks, I may say, were much less inhibited. They used to sally into Lüneburg for encounters with ladies of the night, before which they were supposed to draw a special kit from a duty sergeant manning the PAC, which I assume meant Preventative Aid Centre. The kit was designed to stop them getting venereal disease, and anyone who got VD without having drawn the kit had committed an offence under military law, and was put on a charge. Or so I recall, but it was a long time ago.

The only German town I saw anything of was Lüneburg itself, and that by day only. It was near here in his tent on Lüneburg Heath that Field Marshall Montgomery received the surrender of the German forces in north-west Germany. This was on 4 May 1945, and with typical showmanship Monty managed to give the impression that all the armies of Germany had fallen at his feet, whereas the final German surrender took place three days later, at General Eisenhower's headquarters at Reims. I do not think there was anything to mark the spot of Monty's triumph, and in 1953, when I was there, we would not have wished to give offence to the local people by speaking of such things. The town of Lüneburg itself was picturesque, having suffered no war damage. It had cobbled streets, which cobbles we sometimes tore up by trundling through the town in our tanks. In the Church of St John, J. S. Bach used to play the organ, and there is a very fine *Rathaus*, otherwise town hall, with a baroque outside and medieval interior. That is about all I can recall, except that the prevailing smell there and elsewhere in Germany was a mixture of Turkish tobacco and rexine.

I am not absolutely sure that the tobacco was Turkish – the smell might have come from cheap cigars – but it was not Virginian. About the rexine I am perfectly certain. Many readers now will not have come across rexine, which is, or was, a cheap brown fabric made to imitate leather, which was used to cover the seats in trains and buses and public places.

It gives off a faint but unmistakable aroma, and if you were to bottle that, combined with the smell of cheap cigars, and then uncork the bottle under my nose, I would immediately be transported back to Lüneburg in 1953.

Such were my thoughts and memories some forty-five years later when a man from *The Sunday Times* came to interview me for a column called 'My Hols'. This needs a bit of explanation. Being just a retired local government officer, I had been taken up by Richard Ingrams, the founder of *Private Eye* and then editor of *The Oldie*, in which latter magazine he kindly let me write a regular column. This led to other publications letting me write for them, among them the *Express*. Then I somehow got onto the radio, and from there onto television, including the BBC *Holiday* programme. All of which combined, I suppose, to give me late in life a sort of minor notoriety just sufficient to make it worthwhile for *The Sunday Times* man to come and ask me, 'What do you do on your hols?' and then put the answers in their paper. Being, as I am, about to expose some of the secrets of journalism and television, I might as well tell you now that there are lots of journalists who have a regular weekly column which they are obliged to fill up with something or other, and while a lot of what you read may seem to be a collection of important thoughts which the writers are burning to share with the rest of us, it is actually just what they have been able to think up so that they can get the job out of the way and relax for the rest of the week. It is not to be supposed that *Sunday Times* readers had any great interest in how I spend my holidays, but obviously the man responsible for the column, having cudgelled his brains as to who he could possibly ask this week, finally thought of me, rang me up and came along.

So there we were, sitting in my study, he asking me about this and that, and I trying to give him answers which would be helpful for his column. Then, says he: 'Is there any holiday you would particularly like to go on?'

'Yes,' say I. 'I would like to ride my bicycle down the Romantische Strasse in Germany,' which just happened to be the answer that came to the surface of my brain, and constitutes the chance remark to which I referred earlier.

'Why is that?' he asked, so I told him about the cycling Germans in Greece, and one thing and another, after which he went away and wrote up his bit for *The Sunday Times*, in which all this was reported.

Then, once again, I was sitting in my study when the phone rang and it was the head man of the German Tourist Board. He had read, he said, 'My Hols', and he would like to sponsor me to ride down the Romantische Strasse if I could write it up in the national press.

'I might do better than that,' I said. 'I might be able to get the BBC to put it on the *Holiday* programme. I expect you would like that, wouldn't you?'

The German nation is not, I think, given to wild cries of delight, being a fairly phlegmatic race, but he gave as near to a cry of delight as one of that nationality can manage. So I rang my contact at the *Holiday* programme, and they agreed, at which the German Tourist Board chief was, of course, extremely pleased.

Not so I myself. 'You fool!' I said, addressing myself with that unvarnished candour which I use when talking to myself. 'You have done enough holiday programmes to know by now that if you do it for television you will not have the holiday. The bicycle ride, done properly, takes eight days but the BBC will only allocate four, or perhaps five, but not more, as they never do. They will film a bit here and a bit there, and there will be much loading of the bicycle on and off the back of a car, plus much doing of the same thing over and over again to satisfy the cameraman and gratify the director, whereas what you really want to do is cycle all by yourself from Würzburg to Füssen.'

So then I rang my contact at the *Express* and asked if he would accept a piece about the Romantische Strasse if I were to cycle along it, and he said he would. (I had written for the *Express* before, but never a travel piece, so this was remarkably trusting of him. I should here explain that 'piece' is the word journalists use for what is more generally known as a newspaper article. It shows that you are au fait and up to snuff if you talk about a piece, and I expect they teach that at schools of journalism.) After that, having lined up both the BBC and the *Express*, I had to conduct a little exercise in diplomacy to make sure that all parties agreed to my making the trip twice over. First I would do it alone, riding from start to finish, and so accumulate material for the *Express*. Then the BBC would come on the scene and we would go over the ground again, doing it their way. The German Tourist Board were happy to have it publicized twice over, and the only stipulation between the BBC and the *Express* was that the programme should go out and the piece appear in the press at the same time. This was because the BBC did not want to look as if they had cribbed the idea from the *Express*, and the *Express* did not want to look as if they had pinched the idea from the BBC. When it came to the point, the BBC kept wantonly and gratuitously altering the date of transmission, and the *Express* most honourably and without complaining kept adjusting the date of publication to fit in.

All now being agreed, I went up to London where friendly and helpful people at the German Tourist Board gave me my airline tickets, a map, an itinerary and a book of vouchers for hotels along the way, entitling me to bed and breakfast. Then I went to the airport with my bicycle, took off the pedals, let some air out of the tyres and turned the handlebars north to south, as it were, instead of east to west, all of which is the proper way of doing things if you are taking a bicycle on an aeroplane. Then I flew to Frankfurt.

Rather to my surprise, Frankfurt airport did not smell of cheap tobacco and rexine. It took me some time to find and reassemble the bicycle, and by then the airport was empty, in which state it revealed itself as the sort of place an NHS hospital manager would dream about. There were acres of gleaming, and probably sterile, marble, and plenty of high-class trolleys which could easily be adapted for wheeling patients about. A hint of chloroform seemed more likely than a whiff of tobacco and rexine.

I advanced, quite alone, to Immigration where a gauleiter sitting under a 'Welcome to Germany' sign looked me coldly up and down and said, 'Next time, wait at the yellow line.' There was a yellow line about a yard away from his sentry box, and I should have halted there and waited for his nod before advancing. In Germany, if you see a yellow line, my advice is – wait at it.

Then I took the train, as arranged by the Tourist Board, to Würzburg, which the German cycling lady in Greece had given as the end of the Romantische Strasse but I was treating as the beginning. She rattled off the towns from south to north, but the German Tourist Board had arranged my itinerary from north to south. My impression of Würzburg was wholly favourable and of enormous riches. This great prosperity originated with the 'prince bishops' who ruled it for 450 years. They built the beautiful baroque town, the Marienberg fortress-cum-palace which towers above the river Main, and the astonishing bridge which crosses the river and is lined on either side with statues of saints, plus one known as the *Weeping Madonna*. It all seems entirely original, which it is not, because on 16 March 1945, seven weeks before the German surrender, Allied bombers destroyed by far the greater part of the city and killed 4,000 people in a raid which lasted for twenty minutes. Many of the saints on the bridge were blown into the river, from where some have been recovered while the rest are replicas. Würzburg was, I think, of no great strategic importance but it was a busy rail centre, which I suppose was the reason for its destruction. The restoration has been so skilfully done that I at least would never have known about it unless made aware by a guidebook.

I would have liked to spend more time in Würzburg and in particular I would have liked to climb to the Marienberg Fortress as you do it through vineyards, and vineyards always fill me with feel-good factor. However, I had a fixed schedule culminating in a certain day at Füssen where I was to rendezvous with the BBC film crew, and so next morning I wheeled my bicycle carefully to the right-hand side of the road, mounted, and rode off.

Perhaps I should explain why I was going by bicycle, as the Romantische Strasse can be followed in a car by those who like cars. For those who are not cyclists I will say, as I have said elsewhere, that there is no place from which to see a country that is nearly as good as the saddle of a bicycle. Walking is too slow, and you don't see enough in a day; a car is too fast, and you only get fleeting glimpses of things as they flash by; buses and trains go where they want in their own time, which may not be when and where you want, but a bicycle has none of these disadvantages. From a bicycle you see everything there is to see; you hear the sounds and smell the scents which are all outside a car or bus; you can savour absolute silence from time to time, and if you see something that takes your fancy you can, without difficulty, stop. Put like that, I suppose one might call it the S-factor.

The Romantische Strasse, I tell you now, is a superb route. From Würzburg to Füssen on the Austrian border is about 220 miles, so in allowing eight days the Tourist Board had set me an average of a little under 30 miles a day. Bearing in mind that there are hardly any hills this is a comfortable amount of cycling for a man of my years (sixty-nine at the time), and as there is a great deal to see on the way, the days fill themselves up in the most agreeable manner.

The route is, I would say, undulating, with few real hills. It takes you dipping down valleys, bowling past cornfields, gliding beside rivers, and weaving through woods. Sometimes there are little hills above and occasionally there is a railway to keep you company. There is, of course, no company that I like better than a small country railway, because it means the going is flat. There were frequent fields of sunflowers, which I believe to be almost human. I came upon one patch where the flowers gazed at me with such intelligent expressions that I felt I should greet them in a friendly way, so I rode past saying 'Good morning sunflower – good morning sunflower' as each one caught my eye, only I said it in German: '*Morgen* sunflower – *Morgen* sunflower'. At this they seemed to nod and smile in return.

Very occasionally you are on a main road for a short stretch, sometimes on minor roads, but most of the time on narrow paved farm roads from which cars are banned. Now and again you meet a tractor but otherwise there was no one there but us cyclists. We were not many and it was occasionally reassuring to see a bicycle with bulging panniers coming towards me at times when I was wondering whether or not I was lost.

Lost I was, or so I believe, immediately upon leaving Würzburg. I could see no signs, and I was navigating by map, at which I am not good. I went uphill on an unmarked gravel track which later plunged into a forest, causing me to wonder where I was. Eventually I came upon a little green sign with a picture of a little bicycle and the letters 'Rom. Str.'. I found that these signs appear at intervals along the route, but equally often there are other little green signs of a mysterious nature saying something else. There are plenty of crossroads and T-junctions where you are left to guess for yourself, and the locals, when consulted, of course replied in German, which I did not always understand.

From time to time they most charmingly misdirected me – not, I hasten to say, with any malicious intent, but simply because they did not appreciate that on a bicycle I did not necessarily want the most direct route. At least once it was my own fault because I went into a shop and asked directions but failed to make it plain that I was on a bicycle. By following exactly the instructions given by a kindly lady I shot onto a main road which after a few minutes became a motorway. Getting onto a German autobahn on a bicycle is hazardous, and getting off it is a sub-lethal business, but somehow I managed to get across the roaring traffic to the comparative safety of the grass verge, and then out again against the tide of cars flowing through the entrance. They hooted at me to indicate that I was in the wrong place, as if I didn't know.

From Würzburg I was supposed, according to my itinerary, to spend the first night at a spa town called Bad Mergentheim, passing incidentally through a place called Tauberbischofstein which is the sort of thing that towns on the Romantische Strasse are often called. Bad Mergentheim seemed to have a lot to be said for it in the tourist line, such as a castle built by knights of the Teutonic Order, and a fine fountain in the market place. However, my time was mostly taken up in efforts to find my hotel, which proved not to be in Bad Mergentheim at all but in a quiet country place called Markelsheim, a few miles further on.

I had a corner room with a two-way rural outlook, and from this very comfortable establishment the owner directed me to an excellent restaurant where not a word of English was spoken. The wine was sold entirely by the 250cc glass, and the one I chose had an immensely long name and was delicious. It was the most expensive on offer costing six marks per glass, which seemed to me to work out at £6 per bottle, otherwise not much. I puzzled over the menu and made footling attempts to understand the waitress's explanation, then chose completely at random. The result of this shot-in-the-dark selection was a kind of Surprise Soup followed by the most delicious medallions of pork. I suspect that my friends at the German Tourist Office had sent me to Markelsheim rather than Bad Mergentheim solely with the intention that I should eat at this excellent place.

As I have mentioned my difficulties with the German language, I should explain how much, or how little, of it I knew. I had learnt a bit when a schoolboy at Westminster School, as a sort of bi-product of studying Latin and Greek. Some of the greatest classical scholars of all time were Germans, and it was thought that we should all get a grounding in their language in case any of us turned into eminent scholars ourselves (which I most certainly did not). Accordingly, a teacher with the nickname of Poon took us laboriously through some basic grammar in the tedious way in which he taught everything else, and some remnants of this stayed with me. My method, though, of equipping myself to descend on a foreign country with at least a smattering of their language is to get a Berlitz tape and work through it. *Berlitz Greek for Travellers* helped me to modernize my ancient Greek, and *Berlitz Italian for Travellers* served me well in Italy. Polish is such a difficult language that I did not get very far with *Polish for Travellers*, but *German for Travellers* is most helpful. I think well of these tapes but they all have a peculiarity in common, in that in every language there is a section which is sometimes coyly called 'Dating' but which would more properly be called 'Picking up a Prostitute'. The words which they put into your mouth are these:

'Do you mind if I sit here?'
'Do you have a light please?'
'Are you free this evening?'
'Thank you, it's been a wonderful evening.'
'I've enjoyed myself.'
'It was great.'

Now, there is not enough in the rest of the tape to supply material for conversation to fill the interval between 'Are you free this evening?' and 'Thank you, it's been a wonderful evening.' By this I mean that it would not be much good telling the lady whose acquaintance you have just made that you want a return train ticket to Baden Baden, or that you have an upset stomach, which is the sort of thing the tape enables you to do. I assume therefore that whatever happens in the evening in question can be carried on more or less in silence, though the tape has elsewhere equipped you to ask what it costs and to say, if necessary, that it is too expensive. Others may see a more innocent purpose to this section, but I can only say that it is a passage for which I have never found the slightest use in any language.

It is also a peculiarity of the German language, which I will mention for the sake of those who have never tried to learn it, that the Germans like to keep the verb to the end of the sentence. The English phrase 'I support this proposal most strongly' would become, in the German order, 'I this proposal most strongly support.' An element of suspense is thus brought into the conversation, as until the speaker gets to the end, you cannot tell whether he supports, or opposes, welcomes, deplores, or does something else to the proposal in question. A friend who attended many international conferences in his time tells me that this shows itself conspicuously when you listen to simultaneous translations. When it is the English from French you hear the interpreter steadily giving the English while the Frenchman speaks. When it is English from German, you get periods of complete silence as the interpreter is in a state of suspended animation while waiting for the German to commit himself with the all-important verb at the end, without which there may be no means of telling which way the cat is going to jump. The interpreter has then hastily to gabble through his rendition of what the speaker has just said, while paying close attention to what the fellow is saying now. This must be a special skill, and I hope that the interpreters who have it are paid extra.

For all its peculiarities the German language, at a simple level, is more easily spoken than French by people like me. One does not have to produce those difficult sounds which the French somehow extort from somewhere between the back of the nose and the roof of the mouth. As for the sound of German, Lord Macaulay, in his essay on Horace Walpole, has this wonderful account of Lord Carteret, secretary of state in the government of George I. 'The other ministers could speak no German. The king could speak no English. All the communication that Walpole held with his master was in very bad Latin. Carteret dismayed his colleagues by the volubility with which he addressed his Majesty in German. They listened with envy and terror to the mysterious gutturals which might possibly convey suggestions very little in unison with their wishes.'

If you go to Germany, whether or not you attempt to master any mysterious gutturals, there are three letters you should be aware of, namely H, D, and E. H and D stand for

Herren and *Damen*, meaning Gentlemen and Ladies, and are put on the doors of lavatories. E stands for *Erde*, meaning earth, and is what they put on that button in the lift which signifies the ground floor. I have noticed, and do not think it is my imagination, that German lifts tend to come down to earth with a bump.

The next day I was to ride to Rothenburg. As I rode along, I found that churches were peeping up from villages across the fields, most of them topped with onion domes, such as you might expect to find it St Petersburg. Not, I have to say, that I have ever been to St Petersburg, but steeples with onion-shaped domes on top are what I would expect to find if I did go there, and it was a surprise to find them in Bavaria. This is not something I would wish to gloss over without explanation, but all the guidebooks I have consulted do exactly that, i.e. gloss over it. In fact, not only do they not explain them but they do not even mention them, as if they had never noticed they were there. Luckily the Harris *Dictionary of Architecture and Construction*, which I found in a public library, is more helpful, with this entry: 'Onion dome. In Russian orthodox church architecture, a bulbous dome which terminates in a point and serves as a roof structure over a cupola or tower.' That at least confirmed that I was right about St Petersburg but did not explain what the domes were doing in southern Germany. The Oxford *Dictionary of Architecture* later advanced my knowledge a bit with: 'Onion dome. Pointed bulbous structure on top of a tower, resembling an onion, common in Central- and Eastern-European architecture as well as The Netherlands. It is usually an ornamental top, made of a timber sub-structure covered with lead, copper or tiles.' I feel there must be much more to be said, such as where and how it originated, and why it appeals to the Russian orthodox church, the Roman Catholics of Bavaria, and Dutchmen of whatever persuasion, but not to the Greek orthodox church, as I do not recall ever seeing such a dome in Greece. As I have failed to find it out I shall have to leave you there, with apologies and the comment that the Bavarian onion domes were covered with lead or copper, not tiles.

I stopped before Rothenburg at Weikersheim to visit the schloss, otherwise palace (or castle, as the word schloss does for either.) A very fine schloss it is, with an equally fine garden. Schloss Weikersheim is a renaissance construction, and is full of things and objects such as pictures and furniture and statues, plus a painted ceiling. This is quite unlike the castles in France which always seem to be empty, the contents having been plundered or burnt during the French Revolution. There was a guided tour conducted in German which I had no hope of understanding so I was able to relax and look about me, without bothering to try to improve my mind. The garden, which overlooks the river Tauber is equally renaissance, with fine lawns, at least one fountain and a noble selection of statuary. A number of the statues can best be described as baroque garden gnomes, being jolly little pot-bellied fellows about 2 feet high, mounted on pedestals, carved in stone and a couple of hundred years old.

I made up, on the spot, a little rhyme as follows:

People come from near and far
To see the castles of the Loire
But the castles of Bavaria
Are, it seems to me, superior.

I later recited this to my friends at the German Tourist Board in case they might like to use it for publicity purposes, but they politely declined.

Then I went on to Rothenburg (strictly Rothenburg-ob-der-Tauber, it also being, like Weikersheim, on the river Tauber). The cycling was, taken as a whole, as near to perfect as any I remember. The onion domes lent a touch of novelty and the fields and hills and woods had a kind of placid beauty, not as sensational as the scenery of Greece or Ireland, but more restful on the eye. Furthermore, I was not in danger of being baked alive, as I have been in Greece, nor yet soaked to the skin, as I have in Ireland. Once or twice I think I rode for a short spell on a minor road, but otherwise I felt an enormous sense of obligation to the German nation for allowing me to bowl along on their little paved farm roads in a state of peace and tranquillity.

Rothenburg

Rothenburg turned out to be a perfectly splendid place. It has an abundance of all the best characteristics of the best towns of the Romantische Strasse. It is a walled town, with cobbled streets and half-timbered houses built to four or five storeys in height, the top two or even three storeys being under eaves of great sloping roofs. A friend who had read about it, but not visited it, warned me that I might find it 'Disney-esque' but I regard Disney as bogus but Rothenburg as genuine. Some part of it was damaged by an American air raid in 1945, but you would never know, so skilful is the restoration, and I had no Disneyfied feelings at all. It can, I believe, get terribly crowded but my theory about the emptiness of Germany in August was triumphantly justified. I heard an occasional word of English, usually spoken by Americans, and there was a fair sprinkling of Japanese, but to a man who has shouldered his way through the crush at Avignon in September, and come up against the human traffic jams of Assisi in June, Rothenburg seemed to be very lightly populated.

You must of course visit the *Rathaus* which here is Gothic behind and baroque in front, with a vast tower capped with an onion dome, from which you can see for miles. Best of all is the covered walk round the inside of the walls, about 2 kilometres long. You walk on a wooden floor under tiled eaves, with stairs going down to the town every 300 yards or so. There are wonderful views of the town with its great tall roofs and it is quite like the walk round the walls at Dubrovnik, where you get a similar view of the city from the circuit of the walls. Anyone who happens to have done that walk at Dubrovnik will have some idea of the view of Rothenburg from the covered way.

To digress again for a moment, this was the first time that I had made a trip with a view to writing a piece for a newspaper, and it was a revelation. If you are, as I was, the man from the *Express* you become, in the eyes of some at least, a very important person. If you are spending no money at all, because you are sponsored by some powerful organisation, then you are treated as if you were a triple-multi-millionaire, and everything that can be done to smooth your path will almost certainly be done. It first dawned on me that this was to be the scheme of things when, in a smart hotel in Rothenburg, I was ushered into an enormous room with a vast bed, several vases of flowers, a complimentary bottle of wine and a huge pile of fruit. The manager made it plain that his one wish was to make sure that my brief stay went as smoothly as possible, and if there was anything I might happen to want, I had but to mention it, whereupon everything possible would be done to gratify my wish. I am not used to travelling like this on my own account, and so this treatment came as a surprise, and a very agreeable one at that. I have got quite accustomed to this sort of thing by now, as there was a period when it seemed to happen quite often. I have hinted that I will let you into some of the secrets of journalism, so now I will tell you about the time I went to Canada.

I mentioned to the travel editor of a certain powerful organ that Canada was somewhere I would like to go. I wanted to revisit Ottawa where I had spent three and a half years as a schoolboy during the war. I would like to go in October so that I could see the autumn colours in the Gatineau Valley, which is across the river from Ottawa. I would also like to visit Quebec, which I had glimpsed briefly from the St Lawrence river on board the boat which brought us from England in 1940. The travel editor then snapped into action, and as his paper has a circulation of about three million he did not have to snap very much to produce the effect he wanted. I think they probably made one telephone call, on the strength of which one travel agent and the Ontario Tourist Board and the Quebec Tourist Board in London and their affiliates and associates in Canada set about planning the most superior trip you can possibly imagine, at almost no cost to me and none whatever to the paper.

They flew me to Quebec first of all, where by far the grandest hotel, not only in Quebec but in the whole of Canada, is the Chateau Frontenac. This Norman-French-looking copper-roofed castle-type of building is a sort of icon, a symbol not just of Quebec, but of Canada itself, and I think they have put it on their postage stamps in the past. Naturally the Chateau Frontenac is the place where superior persons, such as the man from this remarkable paper, should be accommodated and so, of course, I was.

So it went on. When I went to explore the Plains of Abraham, these being the battlefield where General Wolfe was killed, a guide sprang up to show me around. Later another guide drove me out to look at the surrounding country. A car subsequently took me to the station so that I could use my first-class train ticket to get from Quebec to Ottawa. In Ottawa the Chateau Laurier hotel presses hard on the heels of the Chateau Frontenac in terms of general splendour, and the Chateau Laurier management, by way of trumping the Chateau Frontenac, gave me an enormous suite rather than a mere luxurious room. This caused, I think, some surprise to the booking clerks and bellhops, who visibly wondered who this old chap in corduroy trousers could be, that they should treat him as if he were Gina Lollobrigida or some equally important person.

My time in Ottawa was organized in the same helpful way as that in Quebec. A delicious lunch in a famous restaurant, a personal tour of a famous museum, a ride up the Gatineau Valley by train and a guided tour of the Gatineau Country Park – these were the sort of activities they laid on. Then I spent one day in Montreal, where a girl turned up who deserves at least a paragraph to herself.

She came, by appointment, to my hotel. She said, with engaging frankness, that she had no idea who I was, but she had a car and had been told by her tourist-board boss to show me anything I was keen to see. This was a pleasant change from all the other people who likewise had no idea why they were to look after me, but pretended that they had, and always arrived with a fixed plan as to what they should make me do. I was only passing through Montreal, and had no particular desire to see any particular sight, so I left it to her, and she took me on a delightful outing round the city, one of the most memorable aspects of which was the beautiful diction with which she described different aspects of the city.

She spoke in perfect sentences complete with commas, full stops and even the occasional semi colon. Anyone taking dictation from her could have got the punctuation exactly right without any further help from her. She said things like this: 'I would like to share with you (comma) Edward (comma) the fact that the Nelson's Column in Montreal is older than that in London (semi colon) older (comma) in fact (comma) by twenty years (full stop).' (Do not hold me to that twenty years – it may have been some other figure but it is the diction and the turn of phrase that I wish to convey.) She was a nice intelligent girl and we chatted in a friendly way. In the course of this she told me that she was engaged to be married. 'My fiancé proposed at the top of the Eiffel Tower and so I had to accept.'

'I suppose he said he would jump over the edge if you turned him down?'

'No (comma) he said he would throw me (in italics) over (exclamation mark).'

Now this Canada trip was not entirely typical, because they laid more on for me than is usual, nor yet is it altogether untypical, because people always lay on a lot. Either way, this treatment gives you rather a rosy picture and creates a bit of a problem when you come to write your piece. Not all the readers could afford to stay in the Chateau Laurier, let alone in a suite, and few would get the individual guided tours which were provided for me, so you have to tone it down a bit when you come to write up the holiday. On the other hand the Chateaux Frontenac and Laurier had treated me so extremely well that I could not fail, in decency, to repay them with a few kind words.

As regards the Romantische Strasse the German Tourist Board acted with admirable restraint. They gave me my air tickets and arranged my accommodation and let me get on with it. No guides popped up to show me around but, as at Rothenburg, the hotel rooms were surprisingly luxurious and the managers all briefed to be as helpful as possible.

He at Rothenburg insisted that I should visit a most terrible shop called Käthe Wohlfahrt which sells Christmas junk and plays 'Jingle Bells' all year round. It is full of baubles and tinsel and plastic trees and beastly toys and that sort of thing, all crammed together so that you feel in danger of smashing a bauble or knocking over a loaded table as you creep around. 'Kitsch' is a word I am not quite sure about, but I think it applies to this sort of thing. Anyway, the people running the store obviously understood their business, as it was crowded and the kitsch was selling briskly with the tills jingling as well as the bells.

After Rothenburg comes Dinkelsbühl and at Dinkelsbühl I upset a Coca-Cola and a waitress. (This is an example of that figure of speech called a zeugma, which I like to use whenever I spot an opportunity.) I find that, after a stint of strenuous cycling, the best restoratives are either sweet black coffee or Coca-Cola. It was a hot August day, and when I got to Dinkelsbühl, before finding my hotel, I parked my bicycle against a medieval kerb of the medieval street, sat down at a table outside a cafe, ordered a Coca-Cola and almost at once knocked it over. It made a considerable mess, flooding a clean red-and-white check tablecloth and spilling onto the pavement. I went inside, explained what I had done, grovelled and apologized as best I could, (the situation is not provided for in the *Berlitz German for Travellers*) and ordered a fresh Coca-Cola. The episode sticks in my mind because of the unreasonable behaviour of the waitress. She was, it seemed to me, quite unnecessarily grumpy. She made an enormous fuss over gathering up the sodden tablecloth and dumping it in a bucket; there was a great deal of surly ostentation in the way she wiped the table and there was much obvious clanking about with another bucket while she dried the pavement. My view of the matter was that these things happen, and that they should have taught her at waitress school, or wherever she learned her trade, that the proper thing to do was to pretend that it was quite a jolly interlude which had enlivened her otherwise dull day, and then dealt with it in a cheerful manner. I also felt that had she realized she was causing embarrassment to the representative of that powerful organ the *Express* newspaper of London, she would have behaved better, but I had no way of getting this idea across to her.

Dinkelsbühl is a kind of minor Rothenburg in its own right. It too is a walled medieval town, but smaller and quieter and with no nasty shops. I walked round the walls, this time on the outside, rather than the inside as at Rothenburg. The path took me past four towers built into the fortifications, including one at a gate called the Segringer Tor which has as fine an onion dome as you could wish to see. Onion domes are in Germany by no means confined to ecclesiastical buildings, as the architectural books suggest.

There is also, within the walls, a very large Gothic church big enough for a cathedral if one was wanted, and with very beautiful fan vaulting to the roof, dedicated to St Georg. The German nation, I discovered, keeps its churches and cathedrals in the good order that you would expect. There is no sign of the damp or the crumbling masonry that often distress me in France or Italy, nor did I see anywhere any scaffolding or other signs of emergency repairs. If there had been placards asking me for contributions towards a new roof, or something similar, I think I would have noticed and certainly contributed, but I didn't, nor did anyone ask me for money to go in, as they do at Ely Cathedral or Westminster Abbey. Furthermore, they do not obstruct the nave of a church like St Georg with a rood screen, so you can admire the whole building from end to end; nor yet do they clutter their church corners with daubs and cut-outs made by school children or with posters advertising good causes; nor again are the walls covered with inscriptions commemorating the virtues of departed worthies, nor are the tombs of such worthies scattered higgledy-piggledy about the aisles. Calm and orderly are the words that spring to mind, to describe the peaceful beauty of St Georg.

Not so peaceful is the flight of stairs up to the tower. I suffer from a sort of obsession about stairs, and if I see some going upwards I feel obliged to climb them. There was no resisting the 200-foot climb to the top of the tower of St Georg, where I emerged panting to enjoy another view of medieval rooftops.

The cycling from Dinkelsbühl to Nördlingen, which came next, was as good as ever, on the same little roads through the same rustic scenery and occasional villages. As usual, keeping on the right track was a kind of treasure hunt. Instead of following the little green signs to find the route, you rely on the map and see if you can occasionally spot a sign. Every time I saw one I felt that I had scored a point in a mysterious game with unwritten rules, played between me and the tourist authorities. Their objective was, I felt, to give me as little help as the rules allow, and mine was to get where I was going, in spite of them.

There is little I can tell you about Nördlingen, not because there isn't plenty to see, but because you've heard it all before. Nördlingen is a fortified medieval town like Rothenburg and Dinkelsbühl; it has a large church of St Georg like the St Georg at Dinkelsbühl and this St Georg also had a tower which you can climb if you can manage 365 steps, so I did. Nördlingen has a covered sentry walk round the walls, like Rothenburg, round which I walked. Indeed, if you started your holiday at Nördlingen you'd be astonished at all this, and at the huge houses with sloping roofs, but the fact that I arrived there after Würzburg, Rothenburg and Dinkelsbühl, and that I did not knock over any Coca-Cola as a preliminary to looking round means that here I am left with nothing fresh to say.

I was, though, getting enormous pleasure every day from the simple acts of arriving, showering, changing, wandering about looking at the outside of things, and thinking about my dinner as I had always worked up such a good appetite. This brings me to the subject of food about which my brother-in-law had taken a gloomy view, saying that there would be nothing to eat but sausages. In this he was, I am pleased to say, wrong.

Every day kicked off with a huge breakfast selected from fruit juice, fresh fruit, stewed fruit; every kind of cereal; every imaginable form of yogurt; cold meats; a great variety of cheeses; white bread, brown bread, black bread, currant bread, croissants, cheese rolls and probably a number of other things that I have forgotten. I think the German nation pioneered this kind of breakfast and then propagated the idea throughout the rest of the world by going everywhere as tourists and expecting to find it wherever they went. You now get this sort of spread, or some version of it, in any reasonable hotel pretty well anywhere, but it was new to me at the time. Having put away a great deal of what was on offer at breakfast, washed down with plenty of tea, I managed at lunchtime with a snack from a bakery or possibly coffee and cake, the cakes, I may say, being of a high standard.

When it came to dinner I had no repeats of the mystery menu of Markelsheim, as adequate English was now spoken everywhere. The German currency at that time was said to be very strong, and I feared that the strength of the mighty mark might be a deterrent to my eating anything other than sausages, as per my brother-in-law. Not so. One thing I can tell you about Nördlingen is that here, by selecting what seemed to be a smart restaurant; by pushing my appetite to the limit on smoked trout, roast pork and apple strudel; and by having a liqueur (*kümmel*) with my coffee, I managed to run up a bill of £20, but £15 or less was more usual.

Sometimes I drank the wine and sometimes beer. My father always professed a great contempt for English beer, which he said was too weak to bother with, so we never had any in the house. There was a war on at the time I am speaking of, and the beer was brewed extra weak to make the barley go further, but as my father never went to a pub and therefore never drank beer at all, his opinion was based entirely on what he had read in the newspaper. This almost total absence of knowledge did not stop him from having a firm opinion that the only beer worth drinking in the whole world was Münchener beer, i.e. the beer brewed in Munich. I never knew him to go to Munich, nor to anywhere else in Germany, and I think the word 'Münchener' was the only German word in his whole vocabulary. Still, he was altogether dogmatic about Münchener beer, so I suppose that at least once in his life somebody must have given him a glass of this brew and he had talked about it ever after. Which being so, I approached my first glass of Bavarian beer with high expectations.

It was a lager, very cool, and as it was draught I couldn't tell the strength, as one can by looking at the label on a bottle. In a beer garden later on I had one of their huge litre mugs and it had no special effect, so it cannot have been particularly strong. There are, I have read, well over 1,200 breweries in Germany, and so obviously there is a good deal of variety, including differences in Münchener beer itself. Brewing is strictly controlled by law and almost all beer is made of malted barley, hops, yeast and nothing else but water, making it a Real Ale. Sometimes they asked what sort of beer I wanted, and the two answers I was able to give were either *'Helles Bier'* which was light in colour, or *'Dunkles Bier'* which was dark and seemed to be stronger. As beer is on tap, in one form or another, at all times and all over the place, I drank a good deal of it.

Beer is a subject on which I feel strongly, but I am lucky enough to have a brewer and distiller as a son-in-law, and by comparison with his vast knowledge I would never dare to pretend to any expertise on my own account. I feel confident, however, that he would have approved whole-heartedly of the German beer, of the multitude of German breweries, and of the strict control of the ingredients. For my own part I found it unfailingly delicious but, having said this, in defence of English beer, if any is needed, let me pay tribute to His Royal Highness Prince Charles, who is not only Prince of Wales but, in my view, prince of brewers as well. I like to think that Duchy Original Ale is brewed under His Royal Highness's direct supervision. I see him in my mind's eye standing in a white coat in his personal brew house at Highgrove, carefully overseeing the malting of the organic barley which has been grown under his eye and on his own estates, and later measuring out with his own hands the exact proportion of organic hops to produce the glorious and colourful result that he achieves. It is possible, I admit, that my imagination is at fault, or even over-heated. Prince Charles is a man of extraordinary talents and the gift of delegation is probably among them. It may be that, having devised this superb ale, he has delegated the actual production of it to humbler hands, so that he can give attention to yet other of his great causes, such as the development of the Prince's Trust, the promotion of organic farming, the rescue of the English language from the assaults of barbarism, and the defence of the common man against town planners and architects. It will be seen that I am a warm admirer of Prince Charles, and I wish to say that by no means the least of his achievements is a beer which can stand comparison with the finest that Bavaria has to offer.

After Nördlingen came Augsburg which is a goodish ride of something like 45 miles. It is also a bigger place, being the biggest city in Bavaria after Nürnberg (or Nuremberg, if you like it better like that) but a pleasant city to walk about. You get, in Augsburg, a splendid mixture of architectural styles. The huge Dom St Maria, otherwise Cathedral of St Maria, is partly Romanesque, but with Gothic towers, aisles and Gothic carvings. There are five eleventh-century stained glass windows depicting Old Testament figures in wonderful bright and fresh colours. I love stained glass. It is one of the few art forms that has consistently produced beautiful work even down to the present day, at a time when most of the visual arts seem to me to be in a state of collapse. These windows at Augsburg are, I read, the oldest in the whole world to remain in their original place. It is a constant marvel to me that such craftsmen and builders could exist at a time of low technology, elementary medicine and a short life expectancy, in which circumstances you would think all available labour would be required to scratch a living from the soil, without any kind of surplus to raise magnificent buildings to the glory of God, or time to acquire the skills to decorate them in such beautiful style.

As a complete contrast to the majestic calm of the Dom, the humble-looking church of St Anna puts on a blaze of colour inside which is about as baroque as baroque can be, without verging into the rococo. To be truthful, I am far from sure of the precise difference between the two, but I regard the baroque as highly ornamented and decorative, but the rococo as curly-wurly and occasionally ridiculous. Whether or not you care for the baroque is a matter of taste. The Germans, the Austrians and I all like it a lot, whereas my wife doesn't, as she prefers a simpler, or at least a more restrained style. Anyway, there is nothing restrained about the chapel of St Anna, which is a glorious display of gilding, stained glass, ornate pavement and sculpture.

This chapel was paid for by an immensely rich family of bankers called Fugger. These Fuggers, in the sixteenth century, also built and endowed a little settlement of almshouses within the city, called, appropriately, the Fuggerei. I wandered into it rather by accident, to find little paved streets of little houses, a little fountain and a little church. The little rent of the little houses was fixed by Jacob Fugger, when he built them, at 1 mark 72 pfennigs per annum and it has remained at that figure ever since, (except that I suppose it has now had to be converted to a couple of euros.) You have to be a devout Catholic to qualify as a Fugger tenant, and I presume you have to be German as well, which is a pity, as I can see my wife and me as a sweet little old couple settling very happily into a little Fugger house otherwise.

It was quite impossible to find the right way out of Augsburg so I got lost, as at Würzburg. They seem to make a point of not marking the route out of big towns, and I only found it with the aid of several pedestrians, a couple of cyclists, a party on horseback and a jogger. When I finally hit the right track I felt that the little green sign had an air of impertinence about it: 'So, here you are, are you? I never thought you would make it.' Once found, the route more or less surrendered, and led me through a wood beside a narrow fast-flowing river with occasional signs on either banks seeming to say 'Private Property – Keep Out.' Then it went along a cart track through a nature reserve alive with butterflies. I loved it.

I had brought with me a cycling helmet. I have no doubt that I ought to wear one in England but I never do, as it is the stupidest-looking headgear ever invented, and inadequate as a sun-hat in hot weather. I knew, though, that the BBC would insist on my wearing one, as the health and safety people would get all worked up and say I was corrupting the youth of the nation if I appeared on the screen without such a thing. I wore it leaving Würzburg, as I thought that helmets might be required by law in Germany, and that I might be arrested without one. Alternatively there might be a strict convention that helmets are to be worn, and I might be hissed in the streets or pelted with stones by small boys if I appeared bareheaded. Once I found the right track after Würzburg I noticed a number of sun-hatted cyclists, so I took off the helmet and put on my hat. I will add for good measure that I was not wearing the peculiar Lycra leotards which some cyclists affect, nor any other fancy gear. I did wear shorts, but this is a habit I have since discontinued, because of my dentist, who saw the final television film and said 'Don't wear shorts. Old men in shorts look ridiculous.' I took notice of what he said, and the world would be a better place if other old men did the same.

How much tourism you do on the Romantische Strasse depends, of course, on how soon you arrive at each place. Landsberg is just nicely situated, being 25 miles from Augsburg, so in spite of getting lost I got there in good time. You can see everything in an hour and a half, which I know for certain as I went to the tourist office and they gave me an excellent map that took me on a one and a half hour walk. Some of it was beside the river, which is here the river Lech; some of it was beside the walls, through which you can pass by a gateway topped by an imposing tower 110 feet tall. I admired the complicated stucco patterns on the front of the *Rathaus* and the fountain with the statue of the Virgin Mary opposite. Most of all I was bowled over with wonder and delight by the Church of the Assumption, where the rich splendour of the decorations made the baroque of St Anna in Augsburg look positively restrained. It puzzles me now, looking back, that I was quite so moved, but when I later insisted that the television crew come and film this wonderful church, I was so overcome by it all that I could not speak the lines they wanted me to say, owing to lumps in my throat and tears in my eyes. The result was that I was filmed saying nothing, which was a great improvement on anything I might have said. I just wandered and gazed, and instead of any words of mine they played music of, I think, Bach.

Landsberg, as I did not know at the time, was formerly a place where they locked up political prisoners, including Adolf Hitler. It was here, apparently, that he dictated *Mein Kampf* to Rudolf Hess. *Mein Kampf* (which means 'My Struggle') is not a book that one would normally attempt to read, though I have since had a look at it. You would need to be a dogged and determined student of German history to wade through the 625 pages of cramped print which came from the public library, the content being described in the Introduction as 'dull, bombastic, repetitious and extremely badly written.' Hitler's idea for a title was originally 'A Four and a Half Years Struggle Against Lies, Stupidity and Cowardice' but his publisher suggested that *Mein Kampf* might be a snappier title. The publisher knew his business, as it sold over one and a half million copies in German and thousands more in translation.

The Preface is dated 16 October 1924, from 'Landsberg am Lech, Fortress Prison'.

Here Hitler served eleven months of a five-year sentence after a brush with the Munich police which left three policemen and sixteen Nazis dead. I could see from dipping into it that Hitler not only had a great dislike of Jews, Bolsheviks and Freemasons, but also that he seemed to think that all Freemasons were Bolsheviks, all Bolsheviks were Jews, and all Jews were Freemasons. I think Hess's sanity was always in doubt, both when he parachuted into England in 1940 and at the Nuremberg trial, and I should think that it was taking 625 pages of dictation of such stuff which drove him over the edge.

At Schongau, which came next, I went first as usual to find my hotel which was, most unusually, shut. I rang the bell, banged on doors, rattled windows and got nowhere. Schongau is only a small place, so I went off to look at it, leaving my bicycle and bags locked to the lamp post at the hotel. I found that Schongau, like other places on this route, is completely surrounded by an impressive wall and strong towers. The prosperity which all these places obviously enjoyed in past times is a striking example of a remark which I had found previously, and looked up later, in the *History of Greece* written by the nineteenth-century historian George Grote: 'Decided superiority of the means of defence over those of attack, in rude ages, has been one of the grand promotive causes both of the growth of civic life and of the general means of human improvement.' The Schongau fortifications were built between the fourteenth and sixteenth centuries, and would undoubtedly have given it a decided superiority over any means of direct attack at that time. I did not explore beyond the wall, from which I may say you get a good view of the Allgäu mountains, as I kept nipping back to the hotel to see if it, or the management, had come to life. I began to wonder whether there had been for once a failure of Teutonic efficiency. Perhaps my booking had somehow gone astray. Perhaps the hotel had gone bankrupt while I was happily cycling along. In either case I would need to look about for somewhere else to stay, but at the third attempt I found the door open and the manager not at all apologetic at having shut me out, though quite surprised at my having got there so early, which was about 1 p.m.

He gave me an excellent room in his otherwise empty hotel, and after I had unpacked my bags the phone went, which was a surprising thing as I did not think anyone knew where I was. A girl with a near-South African accent said her name was Anne and that she was the director who would be in charge of the TV film. She and the camera crew were, she said, already established in the hotel in Füssen where I was supposed to meet them next day. Would I like to abandon my hotel and join them in theirs? If I did, someone would come and pick me up, bicycle and all.

Now, having had such difficulty in getting into my hotel I was reluctant to leave it so soon and on a whim. Also, as Füssen is on the Austrian border and is the last stop on the Romantische Strasse, it was essential that I got there from Schongau by bicycle and not by any other means, or I would not have done the trip properly from end to end. As Anne immediately appreciated this point, and promised most solemnly that I should be allowed, at some time, to bicycle from Schongau to Füssen, it was clear that she was an intelligent and reasonable person with whom one could do business. How would it do now, she asked, if they came to collect me, took me to Füssen where we could have dinner together, and then brought me back to Schongau and the hotel to which I had become so strangely but firmly attached? That would do fine, I said graciously, so a time was fixed at which a German lady in a car would come to get me.

Now is the moment to reveal, or as politicians like to say, 'unveil', some of the inner workings of television. I have often been asked the question: 'Do you have a holiday when you make a *Holiday* programme?' To this the answer is 'Yes and no'. The idea of a holiday implies that you will enjoy yourself, and whether you do or not depends on a single factor which was explained to me early on by a cameraman called Andrew Godfrey. 'It does not matter where you go,' he said, 'it is simply a question of who you go with.' This I have found to be entirely true, having had a perfectly horrible time on the French canals, which you would think would be enjoyable but wasn't, and a perfectly lovely time on the Isle of Wight, which you would think would be dull but wasn't. The trouble with the French canals was a young director who kept calling my wife and me 'Kids'. His great idea was that we kids should be given a cooking lesson on board a canal boat and pretend to cook some foul French dish which we would never have dreamt of eating, still less of cooking, while on holiday. The pleasure of the Isle of Wight, by contrast, was in cycling from one luxury hotel to the next in the company of an attractive girl called Mary and two jolly fellows for a camera crew, pausing to film the donkeys at Carisbrooke Castle and that sort of thing along the way.

If the holiday in question is to happen somewhere abroad, the system works like this. A car takes you to the airport and there, or on the plane, or somehow at some point you make contact with three people who you may never have met before, they being the cameraman, the sound recordist, and, usually, someone from the holiday company. You can spot a camera crew because they always travel with twelve huge steel boxes as well as their suitcases. These boxes are a great feature of the whole undertaking. They have to be counted into the baggage system at the start, counted out again on arrival, and regularly counted on and off the van in which they travel, and in and out of hotels at which you stay, as they contain expensive stuff and must not get lost. Occasionally there is a scene at the airport because it is a fixed rule of cameramen that they must not be parted from their cameras, which are too costly and delicate to be put in the cargo hold, and so must travel as hand luggage. Some airlines refuse to allow this, but all cameramen insist upon it, and the outcome is always that the airline backs down and the cameraman wins.

If you are travelling economy class you can hang around looking out for steel boxes, and so find the crew, but sometimes the holiday company either pays for you to go business class, or wheedles the airline into believing that the magnificent publicity they are going to get out of the programme is such that you ought to be upgraded in order to put you in a friendly frame of mind. In this case you can wander off to lounge in luxury in the luxury business class lounge. Either there, or in the departure lounge, or on the plane you have then to spot two people who look like a camera crew and introduce yourself. Cameramen are, as the name implies, generally male and I have never filmed with a camerawoman, though I believe there are some about. The sound recordist may be man or woman, but is usually a man, while the holiday company representative is usually a woman.

You are met at the other end by yet another person who you may never have set eyes on before. This is the director and he or she has gone ahead to carry out a recce and make a plan. Depending on where you are, a representative of the local tourist authority may join the party, his or her duty being to smooth over any difficulties (such as when the police in Portugal refused to let us film on a beach unless they were bribed). With this group of people you will be together from breakfast to bedtime for four or five days, and if you all get on it is good fun, and if you don't it is dreadful.

The question of whether you have a holiday and the matter of whether or not you enjoy yourself are not the same. The likelihood is that you will be, in some sense, working pretty well all day, and possibly from 7 a.m. to sunset, which does not sound like being on holiday. On the other hand, the things you are working at will be the sort of things that you would do on holiday and are therefore probably enjoyable. This I will explain by reference to the Barbados holiday film in which my wife and I appeared.

We were put in a magnificently luxurious hotel by a long sandy beach, about which we were very happy. However, once we stepped outside the heavily guarded gates we were in a pretty run-down and mildly threatening area, so if we had been by ourselves we would just have stayed in the hotel and swum and idled about and read our books. This being, as it was, a job and not a holiday, the BBC producer girl said, 'You have to learn to snorkel. Get in this car and we will take you to the snorkelling place.' At the snorkelling place a very black man called Emerson took one of us by his left hand, the other by the right, and we three walked backwards into the sea, this being the easiest way to do it when you have great big flippers on your feet, such as you need for snorkelling. Then Emerson taught us how to snorkel. Then it was 'Get in this boat and we will go to the place where you snorkel among the fish.' Off we went in the boat, sploshed over the side and snorkelled about, admiring shoals of fish while the cameraman, who proved to be a great swimmer, zoomed about underneath us with his underwater camera. Then it was back in the boat, and over the side again to snorkel among the turtles, and so the holiday and the film developed. We went in a submarine to look at the coral reefs, we rode horses along the beach and drove about in a hired car to look at scenic bits of the island, and more things like that. All this we did for the benefit of the camera, but it was also greatly to the benefit of us, as we had a much more active and enjoyable time than we would if left to ourselves stuck in a hotel. The director was a jolly Australian girl called Gillian, and she had managed to get her favourite cameraman, the Andrew Godfrey whom I have already mentioned. Andrew Godfrey had got the sound recordist with whom he liked to work, so it had the makings of a friendly party. The travel company representative was a young woman who had given birth four months earlier to her first baby, and was still in that state of motherhood of not being able to bear to be parted from her offspring. She compensated by bringing a big pack of photographs of the infant, which she showed us one by one within half an hour of our meeting. The baby looked to me much like any other baby, but my wife likes babies and was able to say all the right things. I like greyhounds better than babies, so I said the sort of things I would have said if I was being shown pictures of a greyhound puppy and sounded, I flatter myself, properly enthusiastic.

We flew out by Air Barbados, and my wife and I were put in business class, but the other three had to travel tourist. They give you things in business class, such as socks and shaving kit, and among the other stuff they gave each of us a red rose. There is not a lot you can do with a red rose on an aeroplane, but I thought I would give mine to the young mother to cheer her up. I plunged into the tourist class to find her, and went searching up and down with my red rose in my hand, to a certain amount of ribaldry from the cabin stewards, such as; 'Hey, man – so many pretty women! Which one you gonna give it to, man?' Eventually I found her huddled in a corner with the camera crew, disconsolately eating airline chicken while we were still at the stage of champagne and smoked salmon.

This will give you a preliminary idea of what the job can be like, to which I will just add that as a presenter, which is what they call you, you will probably get a little time to yourself as at some stage the cameraman announces that he wants to get some 'Gee-Vees' and does not need you for a bit. A Gee-Vee is actually a GV, the letters standing for General

View, and signifies shots of the surroundings without you in them. While Andrew Godfrey was getting his Gee-Vees we took a trip by taxi into the capital city, which is Bridgetown, where we found not much except a handsome eighteenth-century wooden cathedral. There were a great many memorials to dead people inside, generally soldiers who had been killed by the climate or upright citizens who had been model husbands, devoted fathers, exemplary patriots and, I suppose, slave owners on the grand scale (though this was not stated).

But enough of Barbados, and back to Bavaria. We were, I found, a multi-national group. The Near-South-African-Sounding Anne proved to be tall, good-looking, very intelligent and a pleasure to film with. She had begun life in Zimbabwe but moved to England as a schoolgirl which accounted for the voice. The cameraman, Phil, was an out-and-out Australian who had started on the project of growing a beard, and got about to the halfway stage. The sound recordist was an undeniable New Zealander called Grant, which is the sort of name that people get given in New Zealand. Then there were no less than three Germans. The lady who picked me up in Schongau was from the national tourist board, and was called Christine. There was a sturdy keen cyclist called Franz from the local tourist board, and there was a man with a van called Peter who drove the camera crew and their twelve steel boxes from place to place. Also there was Lorna who was English like me, and a surprise. She was a BBC researcher dispatched to help Anne by paying the bills as we went along and that sort of thing, which is not a luxury directors are usually allowed, so I suppose the BBC must have been flush of money at the time. This group of eight, including me, was twice the minimum, because the director usually settles the bills and the camera crew generally drive their own van. Franz, though, was an enormous help as he later got the doors of King Ludwig's castle at Neuschwanstein unlocked after closing time. Otherwise, there were more people to be got along with, and a greater exercise in diplomacy, than is usually the case.

It all worked fine. The only one I took against on meeting was Peter the van man, and that was because he came to dinner in a T-shirt with a coarse emblem on the front. It was meant to be funny but wasn't, so none of us laughed or made any comment. I glared at him in an unfriendly manner and either this worked or Christine had a word with him, because next time we saw him he was wearing a suit, so we forgave him, and he became one of us.

Had you seen the final film you would naturally have got the impression that I had cycled all the way from Würzburg to Füssen all by myself. In one sense, of course, I had, at least as far as Schongau and by doing it alone first of all I had done a much better recce than Anne could have done from a car. This meant that the filming was done more or less where I suggested, so I exercised rather more influence than is usual for a lowly presenter. I use the word lowly because the presenter is the one member of the team who needs no training or experience and can get by with very little ability.

This kind of filming is known in the trade as a 'shoot', and if this is a military metaphor it is quite appropriate, because it all works like an army platoon on a very small scale. The director is the second lieutenant in command, who has to decide what is wanted, control the operation and maintain morale. This is an extremely difficult job, commonly done by girls of thirty-something like Anne, but you may get a director who is only newly commissioned. The cameraman is the platoon sergeant, on whom the director depends utterly. He is likely to be older and more experienced than the director and can make things unpleasant if he feels like it. The sound recordist is like the corporal with the Bren gun – an unobtrusive role but if he gets it wrong the whole thing is ruined. He is in a position of power, because if he declares that he can detect, through his headphones, the slightest outside noise, perhaps from an aeroplane or lorry or lawnmower, everything either stops or has to be done again. He and the cameraman stick together, and as lugging their equipment around all day is hot and heavy work, they need to be regularly fed, rested and topped up with bottled water or Coca-Cola, otherwise they get grumpy.

The presenter, in this case me, has the rank of private soldier. He steps forward when ordered and does what is required.

When I have been filming it has always seemed to me that I had the easy job, but they tell me that not all presenters take this view. The fact that they are the only ones that appear on screen and get talked about can go to their heads, and they then give themselves airs, become temperamental, and demand to be taken to the best restaurants wherever they happen to be. In one important respect, though, as a presenter you are not like a private soldier, because instead of being shouted at you are flattered. As soon as you do anything, however simple, to the cameraman's satisfaction, he says 'Brilliant!' I think they teach flattery at film school, and it becomes automatic. I remember once that I had to climb a flight of stairs while the cameraman filmed my feet and ankles through the banisters on the other side as I went up. 'Brilliant!' he said when I had done it. In no other walk of life can brilliance be so easily achieved.

Camera crews can also be temperamental. I have known the sound recordist to storm off in a sulk because he did not like the food, and the cameraman to spend the whole time moaning about his hotel room. The worse thing, though, that you may encounter as a presenter is inexperience, either in the cameraman or the director. Inexperienced cameramen film too much, because they cannot tell when they've got enough good shots, so they just keep filming and filming until the sun goes down or some other force intervenes to stop them. This holds things up, keeps everyone hanging around unnecessarily, and is annoying. Inexperienced directors give the presenter no scope, but hand him a script and treat him like an actor, with lines to be learned. Inexperienced directors being young and I being old, they often try to put in my mouth words I would never use, wanting me to say that things were 'really incredible' when they were perfectly easy to believe, or ugly phrases such as 'it seems like he was right'. Also, I once filmed with a slip of a girl straight out of film school who if I said 'as' when her stupid script said 'because' tried to insist that I do it again. This, as you can imagine, was a cause of friction.

There was none of that nonsense with Anne. She being, as I have said, extremely nice and very good-looking, I would have put up with a lot from her, but I didn't have to. She would not have dreamt of having anything so foolish as a script, but she knew the shots she wanted and let me use the words I liked, helping me out if I was stuck. Phil the Camera knew what he was about, and got on with it, so between us we dispatched the film in what I think I can fairly call a brisk and workmanlike manner.

We started where I had started to ride, at Würzburg. There is, inevitably, a good deal of repetition in this business. Either a dog barks or you stumble over your words, or the sun goes behind a cloud, or something else happens to make that shot no good so you have to do it again. At Würzburg I had to come out of our hotel and shake hands on the front steps with the tall and imposing manager. He said *'Auf wiedersehen, Herr* Enfield. *Gute reise!'*, otherwise, 'Have a good trip.' To this I replied

'*Danke vielmahls!*' meaning, 'Thank you very much' – the word '*vielmahls*' being pronounced 'feel-marls', more or less.

'What's all this about a field mouse?' demanded Phil the Camera after I had done it for the sixth time and got it right. He was, for some reason, rather taken with the idea of a field mouse, and sometimes used it as my name, making Australian remarks such as 'Hey, Field Mouse, wanna beer?'

We filmed in the garden of Schloss Weikersheim, and in the covered walk at Rothenburg. The Käthe Wohlfahrt shop with its unrivalled collection of Christmas rubbish was strangely fascinating to Anne, and we filmed there at some length. We filmed the sunflowers with which I had exchanged greetings, and I did my best to compress into a few snappy sentences the history of the almshouses in the Fuggerei. Anne duly honoured her promise to let me ride from Schongau to Füssen, which I did in company with the burly Franz from the local tourist office, who led me on an unmarked path through woods which was, I think, more a matter of his local knowledge than the authorized route. The great thing we did, though, was to visit the castle built by King Ludwig II of Bavaria at Neuschwanstein. This we did, courtesy of Franz, immediately after closing time.

Ludwig came to the throne of Bavaria, which was then an independent kingdom, in 1864 at the age of eighteen. The subject of his life is something that all Englishmen should approach with care, as we are inclined to dismiss him as 'mad

King Ludwig' and this is deeply hurtful to the people of Bavaria. 'Enigmatic' they would allow, and 'eccentric' they could not dispute, but to call him mad is to go too far. Certainly madness ran in the family. His aunt, Princess Alexandra, was perfectly convinced that she had once swallowed a grand piano made of glass. His unfortunate brother Otto interrupted a High Mass by falling at the feet of the archbishop and loudly confessing his sins, after which he was kept confined in a castle outside Munich. One of the eccentricities which grew upon King Ludwig himself was his habit of living by night and sleeping by day. He would regularly decide, late at night, that he wished to go from Neuschwanstein to Munich or Nuremberg, or elsewhere and this journey he would make without ever leaving his castle. The distance to different places had been calculated for him in terms of so many circuits of the riding school, and King Ludwig would ride round and round throughout the night with a mounted groom following behind. After some hours he would stop for a picnic, and then ride on until he had completed enough circuits to equal the distance to wherever he fancied that he was going.

Eventually his oddities and peculiarities reached the point where he could no longer rule his country. His extravagances had run the royal treasury into enormous debt, and he had become so withdrawn that his ministers could hardly ever get access to him. In 1886 he was declared insane by his ministers and removed from Neuschwanstein to the castle of Schloss Berg, under escort of two doctors, a police officer, and a number of asylum warders. At Schloss Berg, however, he behaved with perfect sanity and on the second evening proposed to take a walk in the grounds, to which the responsible doctor agreed, and went with him. From this walk neither of them returned. Next day the bodies of both king and doctor were recovered from the lake, where they had probably, but mysteriously, drowned and their deaths remain an enigma never likely to be solved.

In spite of this unhappy story, King Ludwig left behind two monuments of which any wiser king would have been proud. They arose from his two principal obsessions, the one for the music and person of Richard Wagner and the other for the building of castles.

When it comes to the music of Wagner I freely confess that I am out of my depth. I have only been to one performance of it in my life, and that was *Tristan und Isolde*, to which I went with my wife in Vienna in January 1957. Our main motive in going was to get warm, as Vienna in January is fearfully cold, and we had come from Hong Kong with clothes suitable for a Hong Kong winter but by no means for an Austrian one. The only warm places outside our hotel seemed to be the Spanish Riding School, the Opera House and the underground wine cellars, so we flitted between the three. *Tristan* was, as I recall, extremely long, and the music did not seem to be all that musical. My most vivid recollection is of the aficionados who sat high up in the cheap seats at the side from which they could only see half the stage. Their solution to this difficulty was, I thought, ingenious. They followed the music with the score on their laps and when it came to a point when they knew that a good bit was coming, they got up and craned over the rail in front of them to get a proper view. This of course acted as a tip to my wife and me that we had better pay attention as something important was about to happen.

King Ludwig was by no means the philistine that I am, but his biographers say that he had little musical ability. His piano teacher recorded that it was 'a red letter day in his life' when he gave the Crown Prince his last lesson, as his princely pupil had no talent whatever. Wagner too described him as 'completely unmusical' and it seems that his enthusiasm for the composer and his works came mainly from a passion for Scandinavian sagas and Arthurian legends. As a boy, he learned most of Wagner's libretti by heart and within weeks of becoming king he dispatched his cabinet secretary to fetch the composer to Munich. This was not an altogether easy task, as Wagner, who was chronically extravagant and perpetually in debt, had disappeared. Eventually he was tracked down in Stuttgart, where he was hiding from his creditors, and on receiving the royal summons he borrowed the train fare from a friend and hurried at once to Munich. Once he was there, Ludwig lavished money and every kind of support upon him. To quote the excellent biography by Wilfrid Blunt, which I recommend most heartily, 'Had Ludwig not come to the rescue, the world might never have had the completed *Ring* or *Parsifal*; even *Tristan*, which the Vienna Opera House had written off after innumerable rehearsals as impossible, might never have been performed.'

It was, though, with his castle at Neuschwanstein that we were concerned for purposes of the *Holiday* programme. Castle or palace building became, towards the end, an absolute obsession. He built three, starting one in 1869, one in 1870, and one in 1878, and had plans for two more at the time of his death. The cost was enormous, especially as he conceived and required the most lavish interiors. The money ran out finally and irretrievably in 1886, in which year he was deposed. Of his three castles, one was like Versailles, one was a more modest baroque construction, and Neuschwanstein, the best known, is a mixture of Romanesque, Byzantine and Gothic/Teutonic. It was designed by a theatrical set designer and then architects took over to get it built. The outside is familiar to everyone because it reminds you immediately of *Snow White and the Seven Dwarfs*, which is no coincidence, as Walt Disney pinched the idea and copied it. It is itself white, or nearly so – a gleaming pinnacled building perched on the side of a mountain.

The German lady in Greece who told me to ride down the Romantische Strasse put Neuschwanstein in brackets because it is not part of the approved route but a deviation from it, being about five miles from Füssen. It was lucky that the admirable Franz had arranged for us to arrive exactly at

Neuschwanstein

closing time, as even in the quiet and empty month of August there was a rushing stream of visitors pouring out before the gates closed behind them, which they did as a preliminary to opening again to let us in. Apparently, at peak times you have to spend a long time queuing for a ticket and are then trundled round on a thirty-five-minute guided tour, so it was an immense privilege that we were able to wander at will and in our own time with no one else around.

Having said which it was, in filming terms, one of my failures. Anne the director, being aware in general terms of King Ludwig's eccentricities, wanted something light-hearted about the strange behaviour of this slightly mad king. I, having read his life, was overtaken by a deep sense of melancholy at his tragic life and unhappy end.

As the king was being taken from his bedroom here to Schloss Berg he said, 'Preserve this room as a sanctuary; don't let it be profaned by the inquisitive,' since when tourists in their thousands have been trampling through the room in question. I was in no joking mood about this, nor yet in the throne room, a huge room modelled on a Byzantine church. It is decorated in blue and gold, with a wonderful mosaic floor and a blue dome studded with stars. The walls are painted with religious and historical paintings and there are white marble steps leading up to where a throne ought to be, but there is no throne. Anne thought there might be a bit of a laugh to be got from a throne room without a throne, but to me it was just a sign that poor Ludwig had not lived to put the final touches to his dream. Anyway the throne room felt like a church, especially as an altar would have been quite appropriate where the throne was meant to be, and a church is no place for facetious remarks, or not in these circumstances.

Much the same thing happened in the minstrels' hall, which is in the Gothic/Teutonic style. It has paintings from the legend of the Holy Grail and operatic scenes from Wagner, and there is fine woodwork and much gilding, and splendid views from the windows. There is also a minstrels' gallery from which no minstrels ever entertained the king, and that did not seem to be a joking matter either. As for the king's study, with Romanesque arches, and his Gothic bedroom, the walls having yet more scenes from Wagner – well, I could only think of what he had said about its being preserved from the inquisitive, with the result that, in spite of the best efforts of Anne and Phil the Camera and Grant the Sound, all of them trying to think of something suitable for me to say, the best I could do was to moon about radiating a kind of gloomy melancholy. As I recall, they filmed me doing just that, and put music over the top, which I am sure was a reasonable way of doing something approaching justice to the castle, and much better than any attempts at facetiousness by me.

After that Anne pronounced the words 'That's a wrap.' I thought for a long time that the word meant that we could wrap everything up because we were finished, which indeed it does, but not for the reason that I had supposed. One of the cameramen explained that the letters stand for 'Wind, Roll and Print' which is a relic of a former age when things were done differently and winding, rolling and printing were part of the final process. Anyway it now means that filming has finished and it is the director's privilege to declare a wrap. This leads to handshaking and kissing all round according to sex, which on this occasion was very pleasant, particularly in the case of Anne. Then we went off and had a good dinner and congratulated ourselves on, as we believed, a good job well done.

This was the end of the filming but not of the outing. We were to fly home from Munich next day, and as we had a little time in hand, Franz insisted that we should visit the Wieskirche, for which I was and am deeply grateful. This gem, of which the translation of the full German name is the Pilgrimage Church in the Meadow, stands by itself in a field about 15 miles north-east of Füssen with no surrounding village. It was built in 1745 on a spot where a local woman saw tears running down the face of a statue of Christ. The outside is fairly simple, white in colour, with a steep roof and mountains beyond. The inside is stunning. I have a picture postcard in front of me as I write, and it shows a glorious medley of white pillars and arches, gold ornamentation and a glowing fresco on the ceiling. I also have a photograph taken by Phil the Camera which proves that we struck it lucky and saw the Wieskirche on a fine day with bright light pouring through the windows. This little church has, I read, been declared a UNESCO World Heritage Site, which I think puts it somewhere in the same category as the Taj Mahal and the Parthenon. I think this to be a well-deserved honour, and no one going down the Romantische Strasse should omit the deviation from Steingaden, near which it lies, in order to see it.

Then we went home from Munich, and having, as we all agreed, enough material to make a fine film lasting half an hour, the result of our five days work was a film lasting seven minutes. This lets you into another secret of the television world. Those on high in the BBC are convinced that we all have grasshopper minds and can hardly pay attention to anything other than drama and fiction for more than a few minutes. Being, as they are, terrified at the thought that we might switch over to something else and so affect their sacred ratings, they give you four different films on the half-hour *Holiday* programme, the theory being that if you are bored by the bit you are watching you will hang on in the hope that the next bit will be an improvement. It is not for me to say that I understand their business better than they do, so I expect, in terms of keeping their ratings up, they are very likely right. I cannot but wonder, though, whether we only have grasshopper minds because they have created them by treating us like that, and whether we might, if encouraged, be capable of giving serious attention to a single subject for half an hour.

Between flying from Munich and finishing the film altogether there was one more thing to be done, which I tell you about only to complete my account of the workings of television. It remained for Anne to edit all Phil's film down to the obligatory seven minutes, and for me to go to White City to do the voiceover. When you watch a film of this sort, you will notice that some of the words are obviously being spoken by the person who is in front of the camera, but sometimes they come as a commentary from the same person but from somewhere else. This latter is the voiceover, and it gets stuck on in a recording studio as the last act in the process.

You are given a script and the trick is to speak the words in a sensible manner in the exact number of seconds allocated to them. While you may need two or three attempts before you get it just right, this is not actually very difficult. The only problem you may have is that they may also on this occasion try to put words in your mouth which you would never use, in which case they will let you alter them to your own sort of language. The one time I remember having any serious problem was when some young and ignorant director wanted me to say (I forget why) that Lord Byron had never seen the Highlands of

Scotland. I said that he had been to school in Aberdeen and had many childhood recollections of the Highlands, and had written poetry to say so. She said I was wrong. I said I was right. She said the script had been approved by higher authority and could not be altered. I said I was not going to talk nonsense just to please higher authority. I remember this argument with pleasure as it was about the only one I can think of which I felt certain of winning. I knew quite well that I was right about Byron, and as there was no way that anyone could oblige me to talk rubbish, I was perfectly confident in digging in my heels. There was, as a result, a pause, and a ringing up of higher authority, and a consultation with the BBC Research Department, who presumably looked in the *Dictionary of National Biography* and saw with their own eyes that I was right, and said so. So then there was a re-jigging of the script, after which we were able to get on with it.

There was of course none of that nonsense in the case of Anne and the Romantische Strasse, so we did the voiceover with no difficulty. And now, looking back on the solitary cycle ride and the team effort of filming, they come together as a most satisfactory episode in my life. If I were asked if I would like to do it exactly as before, and to have the whole fortnight again exactly as it was, I would certainly say 'yes', which is not, I find, something that happens very often.

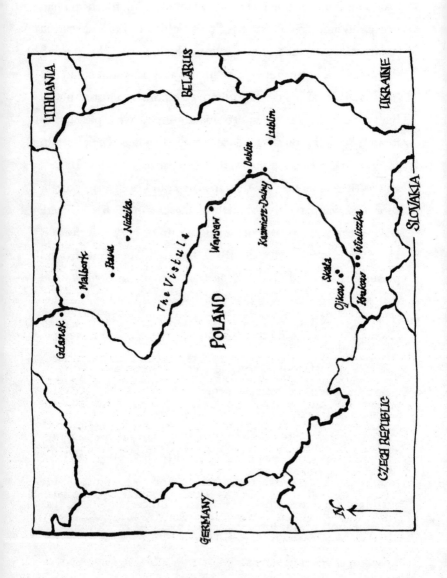

A POLISH INTERLUDE – 1998

Two of the three books that I have written have been translated into foreign languages, one into Polish and one into German. The German rights to the one called *Greece On My Wheels* were bought by a publisher of pornography who was, he said, intending to strike out on a new line. I just hope that his regular customers realize that this was his intention. If not they will have read with mounting disappointment this wholly innocent account of my travels, written with such attention to decency that the book could, in Lord Macaulay's phrase, be recommended, 'as an appropriate Christmas present for young ladies'.

The book about my ride across France was translated into Polish, about which I was particularly pleased. There is a passage in Boswell's *Life of Johnson* in which Dr Johnson arrives in an excited state at the literary club of which he was a founder member. 'Oh gentlemen,' he says, 'I must tell you a very great thing. The Empress of Russia has ordered *The Rambler* to be translated into Russian, so I shall be read on the banks of the Wolga. Horace boasts that his fame would extend as far as the Rhône; now the Wolga is further from me than the Rhône was from Horace.' Well, I thought, when my book has been translated into Polish I shall be read on the banks of the Wistula, and while the Wolga may have been further from Dr Johnson than the Wistula from me, at least the Wistula is further from me than the Rhône was from the Roman poet Horace.

I certainly wondered what the Poles would make of some parts of the book, which in Polish is called *Starszy pan na bicyklu*, meaning, they tell me, 'Old Man on a Bicycle'. There is one passage where, being in Burgundy and thinking generally about wine, I had written: 'I remember a man called Robin Illius saying, "The trouble with hock is that it tastes like ink." Everyone else said, "Don't talk nonsense." "Well," he said, "you obviously don't know what ink tastes like. Not good ink, anyway."' How would that go down on the banks of the Wistula, or, more properly, the Vistula? I imagined the whistle blowing for lunch break at the shipyards of Gdansk, and out would come two workers called, perhaps Casimir and Lech. They sit on a bench, open up their sandwich boxes, and from his pocket Casimir pulls out a copy of *Starszy pan na bicyklu*, and begins to read. Then he might say, 'Hey, Lech, what does it mean – drinking ink?'

'Drinking ink?' says Lech.

'This book says English people are drinking ink.'

'Very funny people, English people,' observes Lech wisely, shaking his head.

'It says English ink is tasting like German wine. You believe that?'

'You are believing that, you are believing anything,' is Lech's reply, at which Casimir nods and reads on.

Anyway, as the Polish people had been so kind as to take an interest in my book and buy it for rather more money than I later got from the German pornographer, I began to wonder whether I should visit them. I felt well disposed towards them generally. Those that had managed to escape the Germans had been stout fighters on our side during the war, and as a nation they had been shabbily treated after the war, so I felt both admiration and sympathy for them. Those that I met seemed to be nice people, but I met very few, because this was before the great Polish invasion which took place when Poland joined the European Union. We now take it for granted that Poland is an inexhaustible source of indefatigable building workers and industrious waitresses, but this was not known at the time I am speaking of.

That it is so is more remarkable than is generally realized. I have a friend whose family roots are in Romania, for which reason he started a charity which aims to improve the very poor medical arrangements in that country. His main problem, he says, is that long years of the dead hand of communism have brought on a kind of hopeless despondency and killed what he calls 'the work ethic', so that if they can be got to do anything, it is only with the greatest difficulty. This is understandable, and one can sympathize, but it has not happened to the Poles, who seem to have more work ethic than anybody else. The two agreeable young men who laboured in my daughter's house were so full of work ethic they could hardly be persuaded to stop for a cup of tea and I can think of a Polish girl who fairly bubbles over with work ethic. She is in charge of the bar at a London club to which I belong, where she does the work of three men. She goes at speed, without exactly hurrying, and brings us what we want by way of food or drink in no time at all. In any spare moment she is collecting glasses or polishing tables or replenishing the bowls of peanuts. She is very pleasant, and she is also very pretty, so one of my simple pleasures is to watch the other old buffers who belong to this club attempting to flirt with her. She receives their attentions with perfect good humour and a flashing smile, and is a decided asset to the establishment.

That Poland could be drawn on for such lovely people was not known at the time I am speaking of, and indeed, remarkably little seemed to be known about the country anyway. I was getting occasional jobs at the BBC, where there were a number of people who purported to know about Poland, and gave me contradictory advice. Person A told me that everyone speaks English and Person B that almost no one speaks English; Person C said there are plenty of hotels while Person D maintained there were no hotels outside the big cities; Person E was positive that the roads are excellent for cycling but Person F was adamant that all the minor roads are cobbled. It became clear that the only way to find out what Poland was really like was to get on my bicycle and go.

But to where? I had to have a plan. One cannot just arrive at some place such as Warsaw and think, 'Where shall I go now?' So I set to work with maps and guidebooks and made a plan which I am quite proud of, as it has an admirable simplicity. The river Vistula is sometimes called the Wisła, with that funny stroke through the letter l, but I shall stick to Vistula. I found, by studying the map, that this river flows from beyond Krakow in the south through Warsaw to Gdansk and the Baltic. It is always a good idea to cycle beside rivers in the hope that the roads will cling to the bank and be flat.

The Danube apart, they often don't do this, but choose instead to go inland and uphill; (nevertheless it is better to stick to rivers than to head for mountains). There seemed to be agreeable minor roads coloured yellow on the map which would take me beside the Vistula, more or less. The travel agent was ready to sell me a ticket to fly out from London to

Warsaw and back from Krakow to London. The thing to do, therefore, was to ride by the Vistula from Warsaw to Krakow and the route I planned was this.

Kozienice
Kazimierz-Dolny
Jozefow
Sandomierz
Mielec
Tarnow
Nowy Sacz
Mszana Dolna
Krakow

I only tell you this because it might help some adventurous spirit in the future. In my case, it was very firmly vetoed by my Polish contacts in the form of Maria at the BBC, plus her cousin Kasia and her husband Radek in Poland. I forget now exactly why they were so much against it, except that they thought, in a general way, that the idea was mad. I should, they seemed to think, just disappear and never be seen again.

I found that there was a general tendency to take a gloomy view of Poland, not just by Poles, who told me that I must keep clear of the east of the country or I would be robbed by Russians, but also by the Lonely Planet guidebook which said that I must take a lock for each wheel of my bicycle as any unlocked wheel would be stolen at once. When it came to it, I only took one lock, lost no wheels, was never robbed, and wandered about in places such as Krakow at night feeling perfectly safe. I got plenty of cycling, but on a different plan from the original.

It was, in fact, the Kasia and Radek plan. They were both doctors, and I had never met either of them, but they were told by Maria to look after me, which instruction they took with immense seriousness. I have to tell you that hospitality towards strangers is an outstanding characteristic of the Polish people and of Kasia and Radek most of all. They had a better plan, they said. This was that I should indeed cycle by the Vistula to Kazimierz-Dolny, but from there go to Lublin, where they lived. They, as it happened, were going to a medical conference somewhere in the Mazurian Lakes, which was quite the best place for cycling, and they would drop me and my bicycle there for a few days. (I do believe that Radek bought a bicycle rack especially for the purpose.) Then they would bring me back to Lublin and put me on a train to Krakow. As getting out of Warsaw was such a dangerous undertaking that I would be unlikely to survive it, they would conjure up someone with a car to take me from my hotel to the station and I had better take the train to Deblin and start riding from there.

All this was conveyed to me in England, and as it would have been churlish to insist on my own apparently crazy plan, I gratefully acquiesced. Whether I gained or lost by this is, of course, unknown, but I was certainly very happy with the Kasia/Radek arrangements. As for my original idea, I have since come across a man who did what I had proposed, but not by bicycle and in 1778. This was the Reverend William Coxe, rector of Bemerton who seems, from the dedication of his book, to have accompanied the Right Honourable Lord Herbert when travelling in Poland. 'I never saw,' he says, 'a road so barren of interesting scenes as that from Cracow to Warsaw. Without having actually traversed it, I could hardly have conceived so comfortless a region: a forlorn stillness and solitude prevailed almost through the whole extent, with few symptoms of an inhabited, and still less of a civilized country. Though we were travelling in the high road, which unites Cracow with Warsaw, in the course of about 258 English miles we met in our progress only two carriages and about a dozen carts. The country was equally thin of human habitations: a few straggling villages, all built of wood, succeeded one another at long intervals, whose miserable appearance corresponded to the wretchedness of the country around them. In these assemblages of huts, the only places of reception for travellers were hovels, belonging to Jews, totally destitute of furniture and every species of accommodation. We could seldom procure any other room but that in which the family lived; in the article of provision, eggs and milk were our greatest luxuries, and could not always be obtained; our only bed was straw thrown upon the ground, and we thought ourselves happy when we could procure it clean.'

Had I read that before, I might have been stiffened in my original resolve in order to see how much things had changed, if changed they had, which possibly they hadn't. If you undertake the long and difficult journey to that Polish enclave of London which is known as Ealing, and if you can survive being misdirected by various Poles and succeed in finding the office block where the Polish Tourist Organisation is hidden, they will give you a map with the encouraging title of Polish Hospitable Farms. It is a map of the whole country with little symbols showing the places, presumably farms, where you can stay, with a code to let you know such things as whether they have television and whether or not you can bring your dog. There seems to be a little cluster of such places near Kazimierz-Dolny, but between there and Krakow there are none at all, so it may still be destitute of every species of accommodation beyond a few straggling villages and the odd assemblage of huts.

As it was, I flew to Moscow, where I was to be met at the airport by an American friend of my daughter who was living there for a reason which I did not understand, but who was called Rachel. I came out from the passport control long after everyone else because it took some time to find and re-assemble my bicycle, by which time Rachel and her boyfriend were getting nervous as they began to fear that I had already been kidnapped even before I arrived. They very kindly came with me to the hotel which Rachel had booked for me, and by way of useful general information Rachel told me that the taxis with telephone numbers on top were safe but those with no number were run by the mafia. This was a very odd thing, as there were a great many mafia taxis openly declaring themselves to be part of a criminal organisation and therefore easy targets for the police, but quite unmolested. I wondered why anyone should take a mafia taxi when there were plenty of proper ones about. It seemed hardly likely that Rachel meant they were reserved for the use of the Mafiosi, and unless I was a member of that organisation I had better not get in one.

I spent the first night in a hotel called the Gromada which was expensive and grimly unpleasant. This was my first encounter with an ex-communist country and it was like being in a spy story. The Gromada had a shabby pretentiousness and a preference for brown paint which were pretty depressing, and there were two prostitutes lurking in the bar who were fairly terrifying. At least, I assume they were prostitutes, and they certainly terrified me to the extent that I was too frightened to cross the threshold of the bar but locked myself into my brown-painted room and went to bed, where I lay for a time half expecting the secret police to come beating on the door, if not the prostitutes. I had, though, arranged my escape by telephoning the lady who was, as part of the Radek and Kasia system, to collect me in her car next morning and take me to the railway station. She arrived in a small car into which we fitted my bicycle with some difficulty, and while it would have been a simple enough, though unpleasant, ride to get to the station by myself, I was very glad of her help because she kindly made sure that I got the right ticket and got on the right train for Deblin. She was also able, in line with usual practice, to give me the most pressing instructions not to take my eye off my luggage for a single moment or it would certainly be stolen.

It wasn't, and neither was the bicycle, which travelled in the corridor. The ex-communist train seemed to be neither much better nor much worse than the usual British Rail affair, but differed chiefly in that the seats were covered in rexine as if we were in post-war Germany. That part of Warsaw which we went through was all concrete blocks, which is as one would expect after the wholesale destruction of the war. At Deblin, which seemed to be a tiny place, I wheeled my bicycle out of the station and began the new experience of cycling through a country where I spoke hardly a word of the language.

I had tried to learn a little Polish, and failed. I had got, as usual, the Berlitz tape, this time called *Polish for Travellers*, and it defeated me. Polish is quite the hardest language I ever meddled with, and seemed to bear no relation to any I had ever met – not Greek, not Latin, not French, not German. I once had a little dabble with Portuguese before going on holiday to Oporto, and while that is as bizarre a language as you could hope to find, at least I could see a certain sense in '*obrigado*' meaning 'thank you', as it sounds a bit like 'much obliged' and indicates a sense of obligation. The Polish for thank you is '*dziekuje*' which does not relate to anything, and I am far from sure how to pronounce it. The tape has got lost, but my recollection is of a lot of sounds which are very difficult to articulate and are wholly unmemorable. The language also is written as if on purpose to confuse, because, typically, the place where I got off the train was written Deblin but pronounced Denblin, and it is frequently the case that the spoken word is not what you would expect from the written.

Apart from this failure to get any kind of grip on the language, the only thing I had learnt by way of preparation for the trip was that Polish ladies, if kissed at all, are to be kissed three times. I was told this by a Pole whom I met on a radio programme. When first introduced, he said, you are to shake hands. On a second and all subsequent meetings the lady is to be kissed on the left cheek, the right cheek and then again on the left cheek. There are now so many pretty Polish girls in England that I pass this on as possibly useful information.

Deblin is, I think, little more than a village. It does not get into any guidebooks, but it is a good starting point for a spell of rural cycling. Those who had told me that not much English was spoken appeared to be right, but everyone was very helpful. I showed my map to a policeman and managed to convey the idea that I wanted to go to Kazimierz-Dolny, so he set me on the right road. I showed it again to another man, and he put me in charge of yet another man who was going that way on his bicycle. We rode along side by side in a state of brisk conversation, he talking volubly in Polish and I nodding and smiling, my one contribution being the word 'angielsku' which means English (I think). He was not at all put off by the fact that he had all the talk to himself, but the moment came when he was to turn off and I to go straight on. We then shook hands in midair, as it were, without stopping cycling, and I drew on my scant linguistic resources to say 'Thank you. Goodbye,' in Polish.

The road was not cobbled and was almost empty of traffic. The country was flat, and from time to time the Vistula could be glimpsed on my right, sparkling in the sunshine. You probably need to be as old as I am to have seen the sort of farming that was going on, with hay set up in haycocks, horses pulling carts full of potatoes and a great profusion of weeds. You do not see, in England, old ladies in long black dresses and white headscarves armed with pitchforks attending to the hay, but you do between Deblin and Kazimierz-Dolny.

It was intensely interesting and I was very happy, but with a slight feeling of 'Poor Poland'. The villages were not pretty and the houses had a sort of ex-totalitarian hopelessness about them, as if there were a national shortage of paint.

From Deblin to Kazimierz-Dolny is about 30 miles. Somewhere along the way I came upon a cafe where I got a sausage sandwich and a cup of coffee. Everyone was smoking very heavily and everyone was very friendly, being much intrigued by the sight of an old tourist on a bicycle. If they had been French they would have been saying *'Bon courage'* and for all I know they were saying something similar in Polish. Certainly they were very ready to smile.

Kazimierz-Dolny, when I reached it, proved to be a fine old town on the right bank of the Vistula. It was much knocked about in the war but you would not know this as it has been successfully and invisibly mended. There is a big central cobbled square with a wooden-topped well in the middle and some distinguished merchants' houses at one side. I stayed very comfortably in an old and largely wooden house called the Dom Architekt, which I had some difficulty in finding although it is in the centre of things. Giving directions to a man who does not know the words for left or right and cannot count is no easy matter. Once established I walked about admiring the square, the mixture of seventeenth-, eighteenth- and nineteenth-century houses and the ornate facade of the parish church. I sat happily by the Vistula sipping cool and excellent beer bought from a stall and watched the people walking up and down. There were boats moored by the bank on which you could go for trips on the river. However, beyond anything else the over-riding impression of Kazimierz-Dolny is of artists.

There are artists everywhere. They set up their easels in the cobbled square and they paint the well in the middle. They paint the houses at the edge of the square. They go down to the Vistula and they paint the river and the boats. They paint pictures of everything that can be painted, painting scenes which must have been painted many times before and are destined to be painted many times again, generally behaving as if they were in Venice. They were all young, some of school age but mostly in their twenties. There is, I learnt, a thriving art school here which produced the famous Felix Topolski, but from glancing over the shoulders of the younger generation I doubted if their artistic efforts would pay the bills in later life. However, I am no judge. They were, I am sure, much more in tune with modern trends than I am, and I wish them all well.

Breakfast next morning was an altogether different matter from the day before. The Gromada in Warsaw had come up with the usual help-yourself affair in the form of dishes of this and that scattered about, an attempt at fruit juice, and

Kazimierz-Dolny Artists

urns of tea and coffee. At the Dom Architekt it was properly Polish. There was porridge and a glass of tea, processed ham and processed cheese, black bread, off-white bread and plum jam. That, as you might say, was that, with coffee, milk and butter the most notable absentees.

From Kazimierz-Dolny to Lublin was more of a rolling road than it had been before, but definitely not hilly. Everyone that saw a chance to talk tried to talk to me. I met a nice old man, old even by my standards, who was pushing a handcart which he had made out of a big wooden box and the wheels of a pram. The cart had a few cabbages and some windfall apples, and he talked to me at great length and gave me an apple. I have no idea what he was talking about but as he seemed very cheerful I think, and hope, that he was happy with his lot in life.

A lot of the farming had an almost feudal look to it and reminded me of the sort of picture you get in schoolboy history books. Strip farming was, they told us, a main feature of medieval agriculture and so that we might understand what this means, the books had pictures of large fields laid out in small strips of different crops. The pictures are often embellished with a pair of oxen pulling a cart and a peasant or two, wearing jerkins and carrying flails. I saw no oxen nor flail-bearing peasants, but the big fields were laid out in strips in just the medieval manner. Some of the strips were strips of weeds, and I could tell from my schoolboy learning that they were being left to lie fallow, which is quite the correct thing if you are going to farm in the medieval way.

I came to the huge and terrifying town of Lublin and telephoned Radek, whom I had never met. He picked me up and took me to meet Kasia, his wife. They are both doctors and both young, he perhaps in his late and she in her early thirties. They were both quite eminent, and indeed, eminent enough to read papers at medical conferences, which is what they were going to do somewhere among the Mazurian Lakes. We had dinner at their flat, which was built, they said, to a good standard for important communists, and was warm in winter and cool in summer. For all that it was tiny, having only a kitchen, a bedroom and a sitting room. From the balcony it overlooked a children's playground which had a rusty climbing frame, a half-empty sandpit and a broken slide.

Two more delightful, friendly and hospitable people than Kasia and Radek you could not hope to meet. Radek is tall and athletic looking and Kasia is blonde and pretty. About a year later she came to England, no doubt to read another paper at some other conference, and made rather an exhibition of herself by casually saving the life of a man in a London club. She, her cousin Maria and I were having lunch when a man at the next table began choking and gasping and was clearly on the point of death. The people with him were hitting him on the back and telling him to drink water, but he was too far gone to hold a glass. Kasia, with the words 'Excuse me, I am a doctor' slipped between them, put her arms round his waist from behind and dealt him several smart blows in the solar plexus. The cure was instant. He immediately came back from the brink of the grave and she to our table, blushing deeply at having drawn attention to herself as she is, I think, quite a shy person by nature. I of course felt that the episode was rather creditable to me, as I had come with a guest who was so eminently useful to my fellow members.

From Lublin we had a long drive by night, and arrived in the dark at a sort of motel, where they left me. They went to their conference and I was to cycle on and meet them some days later. My only recollection of the motel is that, being quite unable to say what I wanted for breakfast, I ended up with Wiener schnitzel, which I do not like at the best of times, and certainly not at 8 a.m.

As the crow flies, I was now about 100 miles, or a little more, south-east of Gdansk, in the province of Varmia and Mazuria. This is an area of 2,000 lakes, of rolling hills, of huge forests and of few people. My motel was near to Nidzika and Nidzika has a fine castle built in the fourteenth century by a body called the Teutonic Knights.

These were members of a German military order formed at the end of the twelfth century during the Third Crusade. They were called into Poland in the thirteenth century by

Konrad, Duke of Mazovia, to defend him from invading tribes of pagan Prussians. They not only accomplished this but eventually wiped out the Prussians altogether and by a freak of history the name of Prussian somehow passed to the descendants of the Teutonic Knights themselves. As so often happened in such cases, those brought in as allies became a menace to those they came to help. The Teutonic Knights, once established, would not confine themselves to the strip of land which the Duke had given them or acknowledge his sovereignty. They formed, by conquest, a kingdom of their own in northern Poland, which they expanded to include Gdansk and most of the Baltic coast. Their headquarters were at Malbork with other strongholds such as this at Nidzika.

The castle at Nidzika is the first castle I had come across that is built almost entirely of brick instead of stone. As I recall, it was empty of contents and almost empty of people, as I think there were only three of us there: an official, a student and me. The official drifted around the place dressed in a white-hooded garment with a medieval look to it, to lend a bit of historical colour and to be photographed by tourists, or in this case, by me. The student showed me round, as it was his holiday job to do this, and he spoke of feasting in the great Knights' Hall and jousting in the courtyard. I am not sure whether he was talking of things that happened in the past or things that they lay on for tourists in the right season, as his English was a little hard to follow, but he was a pleasant young man.

The map showed a selection of minor roads going from Nidzika to Iława and from Iława to Malbork, so I chose one and set off. The cycling was excellent. Sometimes I was riding along avenues of sycamore trees, and at one point through beautiful forest. When I was in farmland the farms had a collectivized look about them, with large expanses of land empty of houses but with an occasional block of flats built, presumably, to house the collective workers from the collective farm. Looking at it, I could see no reason why collective farming should not work, on the once-popular principle of economy of scale, but as one knows, it didn't. Sometimes, though, there were little villages where people seemed to be in a betwixt and between state. Some lived in white houses with cars outside almost as if in an English commuter belt, while others trundled around the road in horse-drawn farm carts. There were old style haystacks and the milk was going to the dairy in old-fashioned churns rather than the bulk tankers which congest the roads of England.

Dinner at my hotel in Iława was from 3 to 4 p.m. precisely, and I only just got in by special dispensation as I arrived at five minutes past 4. It consisted of veal in gravy, Wiener schnitzel, boiled potatoes and pickled cabbage washed down with a mug of raspberry juice which had cherries floating in it. You will by now have grasped the idea that Poland is not a gourmet's paradise, and may not be surprised to learn that breakfast next morning was vegetable soup, cold meats, pickled cucumber and tea.

The hotel was beside a very large lake and that evening I went out to explore. When I am cycling I prefer, on the whole, to be going somewhere rather than just riding around, but this bit of riding around through magnificent woods and sometimes beside water was very enjoyable until I began to think that I was lost. They gave me a map with the cycle paths marked on it, and this was generally pretty clear, but after about an hour and a half I was pedalling along a sandy track through a forest in the dusk, with no idea where I was. This caused me a certain amount of anxiety as I was neither equipped nor keen to spend the night in a wood. I was, of course, worrying about nothing. The sandy track eventually turned into a road which took me back to the hotel and I don't think there was any real chance of my going wrong. Still, as a poor map reader who can take a wrong turning whenever such a thing is possible, I would have been grateful for a few signs to boost my confidence along the way.

Going from Iława to Malbork I passed from the region of Warmia and Mazuria into that of Pomerania. Although Mazuria is supposed to be the place for lakes, they seem to be everywhere in this bit of Pomerania. I was weaving in and out of them, parting from them, getting glimpses of them at a distance, and then coming upon them again. Very beautiful they are but you tend to get sightings of one or other of them in passing rather than a continuous view from riding beside one. Cobbles make their appearance as well as lakes, but luckily only in short stretches through the middle of villages. I was told that cobbled roads were usually laid by Germans during the war, as Germans are fond of cobbles. I can believe this as it brings back memories of trundling around the German roads in a tank about fifty years before, with the tank tracks occasionally spewing up cobblestones as we went along.

Coming into a Polish town of any size is a daunting experience because there are generally a lot of huge ugly blocks of flats with 'communist' written all over them. So it was at Malbork, which was much damaged in the war, and the damage made good with buildings of this sort. My first concern was to find a hotel, of which there did not seem to be any. I stopped two girls and asked them if they spoke English. 'No' they said, that being the only word they knew. One of them was eating salted biscuits from a packet and offered them to me with a lovely smile, so I took one, which was progress of a sort. We then established that they did not speak German, which has often replaced French as the usual language of first resort. We moved on to settle that French too was beyond them, but finally the word 'hotel' struck a chord, and the girl with the biscuits said *'albergho'*. Italian was evidently a language which she could manage, but unfortunately I cannot, and so we could not converse. However, they had got the message and they talked briskly to each other while they led me to a hotel where I got a clean white quiet room for 72 zloty or about £13. We parted with more smiles, another biscuit, and I mustered up enough Italian to say *'Grazie. Arrivederci.'*

The point about Malbork is its castle, which I explored the next morning. This was built in brick, like Nidzika, in the thirteenth, fourteenth and fifteenth centuries as the headquarters of the Teutonic Knights. It is not merely large, it manages, they say, to be the largest brick building in the world and the largest castle in Europe. Taking this to be true I don't see why it should not be the largest castle in the world as well as the largest brick building, as there can hardly be a bigger one outside Europe unless Bill Gates has built himself a castle somewhere in America.

It is certainly vast, and it towers over the whole town. There did not seem to be any English speaking guides, so I bought an English guidebook and was managing nicely with that when I came upon a Dutch journalist and a Dutch photographer who were being taken round by an English speaker. They let me join in, which was acceptable to the guide, a knowledgeable and enthusiastic woman, as she got paid twice for the same job, i.e. once by them plus a bit more from me. Speaking as one who has occasionally been paid twice for the same job I know that it is a very pleasant thing when it happens.

A visit takes quite some time, as on the outside there are huge courtyards and vast ramparts plus gateways, cloisters and drawbridges, while inside there are great Gothic rooms such as the Knights' Hall, or the fan-vaulted Summer Refectory, and a number of special displays. One is of amber which is, as it were, the distinctive and characteristic product of Poland. As gold is to South Africa or Thai silk to Thailand, so is amber to Poland, it being found in great quantities beside the Baltic. When handled it seems like a mineral and is the petrified resin of pine trees. As the exhibition showed, amber can be worked into all sorts of things such as figures and vases and goblets and is, as I later found, the thing to take home by way of a present. There is also at Malbork an armoury on the large scale of everything else, and a great display of porcelain.

I was resting outside after this exhausting tour when I met a very nice English couple who were similarly recuperating. I use the word 'nice' deliberately, although it is over-used and sometimes frowned upon, because I remember thinking that the quality of niceness is a funny thing but that they both had it in a high degree. I cannot explain why, but I took to them both at once. They were touring by car, and when I said that I was going on to Krakow and would have my bicycle with me, they insisted that I must at all costs ride from there to a place called Ojkow. I did go there, and as I had never heard of Ojkow and would never have gone there otherwise, my warm recollection of them may be coloured by the excellence of their advice. The wife had a funny trick of turning herself to left or right when giving directions, and in telling me how to get to Ojkow from Krakow she was spinning about like a top.

Kasia and Radek had finished delivering papers to their conference by now, and we managed a rendezvous that afternoon. We drove back to Lublin, passing on the way a great many people at the roadside selling mushrooms, which spring up in the woods in great profusion towards the end of summer. The great topic of conversation on the way back was the prospect of Poland being admitted to the European Union, which they wanted passionately. The official reason for the whole country being solidly in favour of the idea was that they saw the rest of Europe as an outlet for Polish agricultural produce of which there was apparently a surplus, in spite of their primitive methods. I suppose also it would represent a final shaking-off of Russian shackles. I don't know if membership has helped their farmers but it has obviously been a huge success with any Polish person with any inclination to go anywhere else in Europe. We got back late, I slept the night at their flat, and next morning they put me on the train to Krakow. I could not be more grateful to these two lovely people for their immense kindness to a total stranger.

It is difficult to find words which will do justice to Krakow. All my difficulties with large cities melted away, in spite of its having some three quarters of a million people living there. This, the former capital of Poland and the seat of kings is quite untouched by war. It has a huge, really huge, central square with an abundance of fine buildings and a total absence of concrete blocks. The old part at the centre has something of the look of a university town, except that the spires are of churches not colleges. It is entirely manageable on foot. I loved it.

Krakow has been discovered by tourists, but not in unpleasant numbers, and while they tend to make the hotels full and expensive, they make the restaurants better. There was a English party where I was staying, who were having a lovely time, and I am not surprised.

I arrived fairly early on a Monday, which is a day on which the museums are shut so I went to the cathedral on Wawel Hill. This is a huge Gothic structure of a dark and sombre magnificence. It is more a place of prayer than many cathedrals as there is much lighting of candles shaped like nightlights, and many people were on their knees. While it is altogether free of the railway-station atmosphere which can afflict such places as St Peter's in Rome, I did see three Japanese girls being marched from one tomb to the next by a guide who lectured them in incomprehensible English and from time to time invented some pretext to hold one of them by the hand. The cathedral is very well supplied with very magnificent tombs, labelled with notices such as 'WŁADYSŁAW JAGIEŁŁO, krol polski 1386–1434'. Having admired this particularly fine marble construction, and others like it, such as the chapel of Sigismund the Old and the tomb of Władysław the Short, I climbed the perilous wooden stairs into the belfry to see King Sigismund's bell (DZWON ZYGMUNTA). I did this for no better reason than that a notice invited me to do so. To get to this vast bell, which apparently takes eight people to ring it, you pass through an assembly of large but lesser bells. There is a Dorothy Sayers novel called *The Nine Tailors* in which a man is either trapped or imprisoned in a belfry and rung to death by the sheer volume of sound, so I did not loiter in case the people of Krakow were moved to start ringing while I was up there.

There is an abundance of wonderful churches in Krakow, all in superb condition. You can just wander from one to the next, assured of an astonishing richness wherever you turn in. One knows that the walls and pillars of Gothic churches were originally painted, and I found that they were so painted at the Franciscan church, though the painting is not contemporary but of the nineteenth century. We are all used to bare walls and plain pillars, and I found the Franciscan effect to be somehow oriental and almost overpowering, but perhaps one would get used to it.

The Church of the Assumption is the one they most prize, particularly for the great fifteenth-century altar piece at the high altar. This is of gilded and coloured wood, a 'polyptych' – like a triptych only with more panels. When closed the panels show scenes from the life of Christ and the Virgin Mary, and when open the central panel shows the Dormition (falling asleep) and Assumption (taking up to heaven) of the Virgin. In 1939 it was taken down and hidden, but the Germans found it and carried it off to Nuremburg, and then it was restored to its proper place in 1945.

The museums opened the next day, and I found a fine collection of pictures at the Czartoryski Museum, with a *Wenus Z Urbino* of Titian and a Rafael on loan from Florence as the features of the moment. For simple interest I recommend the Cloth Hall, where there is a display of pictures in every imaginable style by Polish painters of whom most of us have never heard. There is, for instance, a history painting by Smuglewicz, a conversation piece by Kotsis and a picture by Koniuszko in the style of Wright of Derby. There is a pre-Raphaelite work by a Polish Burne Jones called Grottger and a completely mad picture called *Ecstasy* by Podkowinski in the style of I don't know whom. Perhaps the most memorable are two wonderfully sad pictures of Polish exiles in Siberia by Malczewski.

And then there is Wawel Castle, and here I must rein in the superlatives or I will get carried away. Also, I have some practical advice as a preliminary. If things are now as they were then, when you enter the first gate you come upon a kiosk which you think is the ticket office but it isn't – it is the place where you get guides as well as tickets. Ignore it, otherwise you will part with a lot of zlotys (in my time it was 72) to see the royal palace, whereas I went on to the proper ticket office and paid just 9 zlotys. I could have paid 8 more zlotys to see the treasury, but I am not keen on treasure so I decided to miss it. Furthermore, you are actually better off without a guide than with one, because you can pace yourself, separate yourself from the crowds, and find out all you need to know from the notices in English in every room.

I do not think there is a building in the world by which I have been more agreeably astonished than by Wawel Castle. It is a huge sixteenth-century Renaissance palace designed by Italian architects for King Sigismund the Old. Every room is beautifully furnished, generally with wood from the sixteenth or seventeenth centuries, which cries out for you to stroke it. I usually think that tapestries are boring, but Wawel Castle is built for tapestries – the walls demand tapestries and tapestries there are of every kind. There are hunting scenes, scenes from nature, classical scenes, biblical scenes. I found I was standing and studying them carefully instead of rushing past as I usually do. The floors are marvellous, the ceilings wonderful, the painted friezes fascinating, the pictures lovely. Two hours vanished in no time.

In one room there were two young people in medieval dress, he furnished with a mandolin or similar instrument, and she provided with a lovely voice. He played more or less continuously and she from time to time burst into song, easily filling the wonderful room with sound. Old men cry easily and she reduced me to tears. I waited until a good crowd had arrived and then strode boldly forward and put 5 zlotys in the mandolin case provided for the purpose – an example which I am pleased to say was widely followed.

From Krakow you must visit the famous salt mines. 'What famous salt mines?' do I hear?

Why, one of the wonders of the world specially sponsored by UNESCO as a World Cultural Heritage Site to rank with the pyramids and the Taj Mahal. They are at Wieliczka, 15 kilometres from Krakow. Everybody goes there, including the Reverend William Coxe, he whose account of the road from Krakow to Moscow I quoted before: 'Upon our arrival at Wielitika,' he says, 'we repaired to the mouth of the mine. Having fastened three separate hammocks in a circle round the great rope that is employed in drawing up the salt, we seated ourselves in a commodious manner: and were let down gently, without the least apprehension of danger, about 160 yards below the first layer of salt. Quitting our hammocks, we passed a long and gradual descent, sometimes through broad passages or galleries capable of admitting several carriages abreast; sometimes down steps cut in the solid salt, which had the grandeur and commodiousness of the staircase in a palace. We each of us carried a light, and several guides preceded us with lamps in their hands: the reflection of these lights upon the glittering sides of the mine was extremely beautiful, but did not cast that luminous splendour which some writers have compared to the lustre of precious stones.'

There are tours available from Krakow but I got to the salt mines by the public minibus from the bus station. Presumably in a tourist group you are guided in English, but we who just paid our entrance fee were harangued in Polish by a man in miner's uniform, so it was lucky that we had a young English-speaking Pole among us who rendered the gist of it into English for the benefit of an American, a Canadian and me.

It is pretty much as described by Mr Coxe, except that you do not go down in a hammock any more, the passages did not seem quite so wide, and it is all lit by electricity instead of miners' lamps. Instead of the hammocks, you plunge down an enormous number of steps. You trot along behind the miner in charge through passages and galleries, and every time he sees a flight of steps he goes dashing down it. Now and again he stops to tell you something about salt mining and then he spots some more steps and immediately goes charging down again. In all you walk about 2 kilometres and it takes two hours.

The salt miners of Wieliczka, instead of playing in brass bands like their coalmining British counterparts, went in for carving in salt. Rock salt in its natural state is full of impurities which make it black, and the miners had a great liking for garden gnomes, so a lot of the time you seem to be looking at black garden gnomes made out of salt. It was a working mine for 700 years, but the parts you see are a sort of combined showpiece of rooms and chapels and monuments and statues and gnomes, all hewn or carved by hand out of salt. The great triumph is the Chapel of the Blessed Kings, which is almost a cathedral, over 50 metres long, lit with chandeliers of white purified salt. It has brilliant carvings, such as a *Flight into Egypt*, and the finest is a copy of Leonardo's *Last Supper* with an extraordinary illusion of depth and perspective. This was completed in 1927 and so is later than anything seen by the Reverend Mr Coxe.

The Chapel comes at the end, and as you have been going down ever since you started you are now wondering how ever you are going to get out. The secret they keep from you is that you do not have to climb up again, but go rattling up to the top, packed eight at a time in a miners' lift.

The place about which the eminently nice people at Malbork had been so enthusiastic is spelt Ojkow and pronounced 'Oi-tsoof', which is how they do such things in Poland. It is about 25 kilometres north-west of Krakow, and with some helpful instructions from the man in the tourist office and much more help in Polish from a number of pedestrians I managed to get to a place spelt Skała and probably pronounced Skawa. From there I got to Ojkow without difficulty and a wonderful place it is, a village set in a most beautiful national park. A river called the Pradnik runs through a valley of limestone rocks, with an abundance of beech, sycamore, oak, hornbeam and willow. On 18 September, when I was there, the autumn colours were just beginning, and ten days later they must have been magnificent. By the river there are pinnacles of rock like giant's teeth, a little reminiscent of the Meteora in Greece, which are similar but larger pinnacles and have monasteries on the top.

Ojkow was a different Poland altogether from any I had seen before. It has, for a start, an air of quiet prosperity. The houses are large handsome wooden constructions looking as if they were of some age but which have clearly escaped the ravages of war. The key word here is NOCLEGI, which you see written up outside the houses. I was equipped with a word which is spelt *pokoj* and pronounced 'pok-wee' and means 'room' but no one was advertising *pokojs* anywhere. However, I asked a woman outside a *noclegi* house where I

Rock at Ojkow

could get a *pokoj* and she said 'in there' as apparently a *noclegi* is just as much a room to let as a *pokoj*. The house belonged to an agreeable and amusing man who had spent twelve years in Canada as a 'superintendent' or otherwise, he said, 'janitor' of a block of flats and therefore spoke good English. He had just come back to Poland to see his first proper 'fall' in twelve years. Apparently the autumn colours in Ojkow are superior to those anywhere in Canada, but you may need to see them through Polish eyes to get to such a pitch of enthusiasm.

There are people with whom one has but a brief acquaintance and yet they stick fast in the memory, and he is one such. He was so utterly content. He had served his twelve years of janitordom in Canada and, I suppose, accumulated enough money to return to an area which he clearly loved, and to live quietly there, supplementing whatever other income he had by the letting of *noclegis*.

This certainly did not amount to riches. My hotel in Krakow had cost me about £32 per night without breakfast, and my excellent *noclegi* cost £5 without breakfast but with the use of a kitchen. If there had been anyone else there I think I would have had to share the kitchen and bathroom with up to five others, but there wasn't and so I didn't. Those without bicycles can get to Ojkow by bus and no one with a hired car should miss it. It is a place for walking and cycling, both of which I did with enormous pleasure. I stayed for two nights and could gladly have stayed for a good many more.

There are five walks in the woods, all colour coded and clearly marked. You can get a good little book in English which guides you through them. In a madly optimistic way the guide says that all five walks could be done in a day, but when you add their estimated times together they amount to ten hours of solid walking without stopping to look at anything. Just as anyone with a taste for armour should visit Poland because of the extensive armouries at Wawel and Malbork castles, so anyone keen on bats should visit Ojkow as there are said to be ten species lurking in the limestone caves. Likewise birdwatchers are well catered for, with 120 species of birds provided in the woods. The leaflet also said that there were wild boars, and I hoped to meet one but didn't. Instead, I came upon a fish farm which was like seven swimming pools fed by torrents gushing off the hillside. It was filled with black fish called, said the notice, SALMO GAIRDNERI, all leaping about with great energy in the evening sunlight.

There is in these amazing parts a suitably amazing building called Pieskowska Skała Castle. I went to it with no special expectations except to enjoy the 7-kilometre spin on my bicycle which got me there, and came away astounded. I am not sure why it exists at all – it just appears among the wonderful woods. It dates from about 1600. You go in through an outer courtyard to an inner courtyard and then they make you take your shoes off. This is because the floor of the museum is made of such exquisite wood that it is not to be walked on in the normal way, and there is a big box of slippers outside for you to put on. There are only three rooms to the museum, and the exhibition is of bronzes, tapestries, pictures and furniture from the mid-fourteenth to the mid-nineteenth centuries. Being now rather into tapestries I was particularly struck with one of a dog poking its nose into a basket of builder's tools. Then, when you have got your shoes back, there are some two-tier internal cloisters to visit and an ornate and colourful Italian garden which you can see from above but are not allowed into. I revelled in it all, and got wet cycling back in a light shower that came on without notice.

To cap it all, I had, that evening, a memorable pork chop. It is, I think, the only memorable pork chop of my life. I have had individually memorable beef steaks and meals that were memorable as a whole but I do not recall a pork chop such as this one. I had found a pretty good restaurant in Krakow called Gulliver, but I did not expect much in Ojkow beyond Wiener schnitzel and raspberry juice, so on the first night I fed myself somehow in the kitchen of my *noclegi*. Then, on the second night, I ventured into a simple little place in a good position by the river and they brought me a tall glass of beautiful beer and this most sumptuous pork chop. It was tender and juicy, cooked in garlic and swathed in mushrooms, coated with gravy and surrounded by crisply browned potatoes. If ever a pork chop achieved perfection, that one did.

The next day was given to riding the 25 kilometres back to Krakow, weaving my way through the city and out onto the road to the airport, which is another 15 kilometres from the centre. My flight was to leave very early on the following morning, which might have been a problem if I had had to ride all the way from Krakow in the dark. This difficulty was solved by the ever-resourceful Kasia and Radek who knew of a bed and breakfast place a couple of kilometres from the airport, into which they booked me by telephone. I arrived that evening to be greeted with a typical display of Polish hospitality because they showed not the least surprise that I had come on quite the wrong day, but quietly got my room ready, and only later revealed that I had been expected next day. On the well-known military principle that time spent in reconnaissance is never wasted, I thought I would ride the short distance to the airport in the daylight to make sure that I did not get lost in the dark next morning, and the son of the house, aged perhaps fourteen, insisted on coming with me to show me the way.

There may have been a landlord at this house but I do not remember him, only the landlady, because she was very sweet. As I was to leave so early I paid my bill that night and borrowed an alarm clock, meaning to slip out of the house before dawn without disturbing anyone. This was the agreed plan, but when the alarm had gone off and I had got dressed I found the landlady drifting about in her dressing gown, waiting to give me a cup of tea. I drank it gratefully and then we parted. Now, we had first met the evening before and we had shaken hands in the correct manner so this now was our second meeting, but I am not sure that the normal rules of etiquette quite covered our situation, it being dark and she being in a dressing gown. It may not have been exactly proper for me to take this delightful dressing-gown-clad lady and kiss her on the left cheek and then on the right and then again on the left, but she appeared to think it was the most natural thing in the world and raised no objection so perhaps it was quite correct. Anyway, it set me off on the road to the airport in a cheerful frame of mind.

Krakow airport has character, and you cannot say that for many airports. It is small and simple, not a great garish Heathrow sort of thing, and everyone seemed to be pleased to see me and delighted with the bicycle. Also, I had created a problem which an airline girl solved in a pleasantly Polish manner. Somewhere earlier in my travels, possibly at Iława, I had had a clearing out of papers and thrown some odd bits into the wastepaper basket. The chambermaid had come running after me as I left, clearly doubting that I meant to dispose of all of it, but I assured her that I did, at which she looked surprised but as if it was not for her to argue. She was right and I was wrong, because among the other stuff I had thrown away my return airline ticket. I rang through to England from Krakow and the airline people said they would arrange for a new ticket to be issued at the airport, which would cost me £25. At the airport I explained the problem to a girl who began working through a difficult process on a computer. Whether the computer was giving trouble or the process was too complicated I do not know, but after a couple of minutes she smiled sweetly, said 'it is too difficult' and gave me a new ticket for nothing. So I went on my way rejoicing.

Thus it is that I can tell you that Poland is an excellent place for cycling and not all the roads are cobbled; that the people are wonderfully friendly and not all of them speak English, and that the countryside is often lovely and the towns frequently grim. I have never been to Prague, but I have the impression that it has been ruined by English hooligans on stag nights. Krakow, on the other hand I think of as a similar city but it was (and I hope still is) untouched by hooligans. While I can see no reason why anyone should want to translate this book into Polish, as they did my French one, if they did I would most happily spend the royalties on a longer visit to Krakow and a lingering stay in Ojkow.

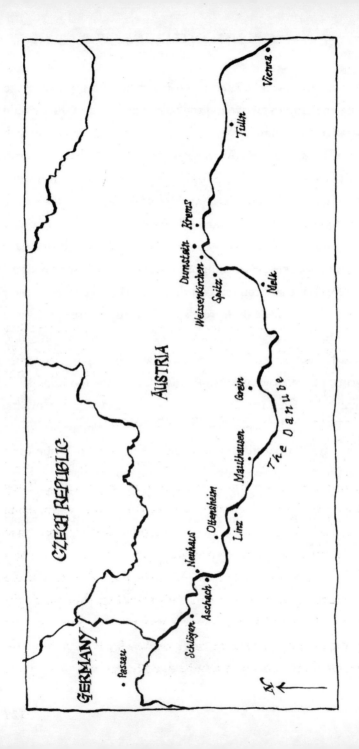

THE DANUBE – 2006

I rode by the Danube from Passau to Vienna for no other reason than that I wanted to do it. I was not commissioned by *The Mail on Sunday*, although I put the idea to them, but they declined it. There was no camera crew in the offing, because I had long since been dropped by the BBC from its *Holiday* programme, for being too old.

Having just started, I will break off for a moment to say that in this they were, I think, in some sense wrong. They might well have been right to get rid of me, as someone they had had enough of. I have no great feelings about age discrimination, being well aware that we old people can be a frightful nuisance and often need to be pushed aside to make room for someone younger. This thinking, though, ought not to be applied to television programmes about people going on holiday because going on holiday is something old people do in enormous numbers. Although it is many years since I last appeared, I am still occasionally stopped by some elderly person who says, 'I did like seeing you on the *Holiday* programme because if it was the sort of holiday that you seemed to enjoy, then it might be something that I might like as well.' That seems reasonable, and when you consider that the whole of the immensely successful Saga organisation is founded on the idea of sending elderly people off on holiday, you might think that we ancients ought to figure largely on the screen, in place of young people roaring up and down swimming pools, which is what you usually see.

But I digress, though I do not repine. I was truly glad to be able just to make the trip for my own amusement, without having to write or do anything to please anyone else. My only difficulty was in finding out how to do it. Once this was solved, it was easy.

I was by now quite seriously old, or seventy-seven, to be precise. I had a sort of reluctance at this age to face the business of getting my bicycle to Heathrow, taking it partly to bits, putting it together at the other end and grappling with the minor damage which airlines habitually inflict upon bicycles given into their care. I imagined myself at railway stations searching for ticket offices, waiting for trains, missing connections and floundering about in the dark in the middle of an unhelpful population of whose language I spoke little. These were all things which at a mere sixty-five or even seventy I had taken in my stride but now I wondered if I should not find it all rather taxing. An easier way of doing things might be better, if I could find one.

My ride down the Romantische Strasse had been on offer to the world at large as a package, with flight, bicycle, route and accommodation all provided. Such an arrangement would suit me very well for the Danube ride provided I did not have to do it in company with other people. As I have explained, I have a great aversion to Englishmen abroad, and if ever I get involved in a group of them it is always a disaster. My fellow men are, in my observation, a mixed bunch. Some are very nice and some are very nasty, some are very bright and some are very boring, and when my wife and I enrol on any kind of a group holiday the nice and bright immediately cry off and the boring and nasty instantly enlist. I do not know why it should be so, but each time we tried it, it was so.

There was a pair, on one of these trips, to whom we took such a violent dislike that the business of avoiding them became the main feature of the holiday. My memory of it is not so much of temples and scenery as of meals at which our great wish was not to sit next to this dreadful couple. In this we seemed always to fail. One of the penalties of being part of a group is that you are obliged to eat with the rest of the group, and if we came in early, these two came and sat next to us; if we came in late, the only empty places were next to them, as everyone else felt the same as we did. I sometimes envy people like the late Robert Maxwell who was able to be outrageously rude without worrying, and it is a great weakness in my character that I cannot do it. Neither can my wife, so we put a brave face on it throughout all the long ten days of this expensive holiday, and behaved as if we liked them.

To see if I could avoid all danger of anything like that and get a solitary package designed for an unsociable fellow such as me, the obvious step was to apply to my friends at the German Tourist Office, but they had vanished. At the time that I went down the Romantische Strasse they had had a London office with chairs, a counter, a helpful young man and piles of leaflets. There was also a senior person somewhere in the background. It was possible to sit down and talk to a well-informed human being, but all that had been swept away leaving behind only a telephone number. This looked like an ordinary English telephone number but it connected me to a girl in Germany. She, though pleasant, was no help at all, being unable to tell me anything except that they no longer had an office in London, which was something I had discovered for myself.

As by far the greater part of the ride by the Danube is in Austria rather than Germany, this would not have mattered if the Austrians had had a proper office, but they too had no more than an English-looking telephone number which put me through to a girl in Vienna. She sent me a brochure of a company which offered all sorts of cycling holidays in Austria, but everything was in German, and they did not have an agent in England. She also said in her covering letter that she would like me to send her £3. This was phrased with the utmost delicacy. It was entirely up to me, she said, whether I gave her £3 or not (and indeed I could not see how payment could be enforced.) If I would rather cling on to my money, then I should do so but if I felt able to contribute this amount towards their expenses, the gesture would be appreciated. I sent her a cheque, of course, but I suspect that by the time the bank had levied its minimum charge for turning £3 into euros, and deducted a further amount for their trouble in receiving what was left, I fear that precious little will have survived towards the costs of the helpful girl in Vienna.

It was, nevertheless, money well spent, because the brochure she sent me was the key to everything. It had a number of different versions of cycling holidays by the Danube, some with bits done by boat and others with bits by bus but generally most of it done by bike. What I could understand clearly, there being no language barrier, were the little maps. These gave the names of the places where people would stay if they signed up for one tour or another. I only needed to make a selection of these at reasonable distances apart, and I would have the route that I needed.

So I did that, and made a list of the Danube towns similar to that of the towns on the Romantische Strasse made on a table napkin by the German lady who appears at the very beginning of this book:

Passau

Schlögen

Linz

Mauthausen

Grein

Melk

Weissenkirchen

Krems

Tulln

Vienna

I got a Michelin map of Austria which was of enormous size and just the sort of thing that would blow about in the wind and refuse to fold up when required. In order to defeat this vicious tendency, which is inherent in this sort of map, I took it to the public library where they had just acquired the latest thing in photocopiers, and with the help of one of the amazingly skilled and talented librarians who are employed by West Sussex County Council, I got those parts of it which covered my route, printed in colour and enlarged, onto three manageable sheets of paper, size A3.

So I was now fully equipped, and you may think I have made heavy weather of getting to this point. If you are the sort of person who believes in the Internet you will ask, 'Why didn't you look on the net?' I did, but then again, I didn't. I didn't because I cannot, as I haven't got the equipment and don't know how to do it. I did because I have a daughter who knows all about it, and she printed out for me a useless sheet of A4 which said nothing that I had not already discovered from an ordinary guidebook. I also telephoned an organisation called the Cyclists' Touring Club and asked the man in charge if, among the enormous number of volumes that they have published, there was a guide to the Danube. He replied that there was no such guide, although he knew that it was a world-famous cycle route. Why didn't I look on the Internet? Which, as you know, I already had, by proxy.

In spite of my apprehensions, getting from Sussex to Passau proved to be, in an old-fashioned phrase, as easy as winking. At Heathrow the cooperative and friendly Lufthansa airline absolutely welcomed my bicycle, which is not always the case. The plane to Munich took off and arrived on time. My panniers came off the carousel in good order, and I looked around to find that the bicycle had materialized as if by magic and was lying on its side in the middle of the fairway, waiting for me to pick it up. The railway station was just across the road from the airport, and the ticket clerk sold me tickets through to Passau, at €20 for me and €4 for the bicycle. A commuter train took me by stages from the airport to the Munich Hauptbahnhof where the train for Passau was waiting. So, far from there being any difficulty about my bicycle the train had a special carriage devoted entirely to bicycles, with racks on which they were hung by the front wheel. I could see this carriage from where I sat, and while I was the only one to go all the way from Munich to Passau, there was much coming and going by other cyclists as the train made its leisurely way along, stopping frequently for their convenience.

As I sat on this train there came back to me a story of an episode on another train in Germany told to my parents and me by a friend of theirs called Robson Scott. Robson was a fine German scholar and fluent in the language. He told us that before the war he was once travelling on a German train, which in those days were divided into compartments. There was only one other person in the same compartment, who was also obviously an Englishman, but being English they did not speak. At least, they did not speak until the train was drawing into a station where the other man was going to get out. As he gathered his things together, this other man turned to Robson and said, 'Do you speak German?'

'Yes,' said Robson.

'Can you tell me the German for narcotic drugs?'

'*Narkotische Drogen.*'

'Thank you,' said the man, and vanished into the night.

That seems to me to have the germ of a most exciting novel to be made into a most exciting film. In the film, as the titles roll, these two men can be seen sitting in their compartment, eyeing each other occasionally from behind their books or round their newspapers, with no words spoken until the train approaches the station. Then the conversation takes place, the man departs and Robson raises his eyebrows (or perhaps contracts them into a puzzled frown, depending on the actor's eyebrows and ability) and goes back to his book. Two days later a picture appears in the paper of this strange other man, who has been found hanged from one of the Danube bridges, or else fished out of the river with his feet in concrete boots. Robson dutifully responds to the police appeal for information and is at once caught up in a web of intrigue (what else?) involving drugs, prostitution, MI6 and the Bank of England. The only thing that prevents me from writing such a ripping yarn is an unfortunate lack of talent for this kind of thing, but anyone else who fancies it is welcome to the plot.

My own journey to Passau passed without any exciting episode, and once there I asked two of my fellow travellers where I could find a hotel. They, with great pleasure at being able to give so prompt and obviously satisfactory an answer, pointed to a large building with a blue roof about 50 yards away. 'That,' they said, 'is a hotel specially for cyclists,' so there I went.

It was beside the Danube, and I paused to look at the wide brown fast-flowing river with some satisfaction. My bicycle and I had reached its banks at Passau in Germany from Billingshurst in Sussex in just under twelve hours without any difficulty or discomfort on the way, and here was a hotel ideally suited to receive us.

Had they a single room?

Yes they had, which was encouraging.

How much would it be?

Including breakfast it would cost €30 a night which was a little over £20 – a reasonable amount.

'I would like a room for two nights.'

Very well, and please would I pay in advance.

Now that, perhaps, should have made me hesitate a little, but having got thus far I did not like to draw back so I meekly handed over €60. My bicycle was put into a huge locked cage with half a dozen other bicycles, and I was given a key and directed to my room, which was a great distance away down a long corridor.

If you, who read these pages, are a cyclist, then there is no reason why you should not do exactly as I did, but I would advise you to have a look at the room first. In calling it a room I give it a sort of courtesy title, but it would be more accurate to call it a cell. While I have yet to see the inside of a cell in an English prison, my impression from television is that such cells are a lot more comfortable than this one at Passau, and to call it monastic would be to imply a greater degree of discomfort than I think most monasteries require.

Inside and opposite the door was a small window which looked out onto the Danube. Under this window was a wall-to-wall bed. The head was under the window, the foot towards the door, and the bed itself enclosed on either side by the walls of the cell. If, on a generous interpretation, I say that the bed was 3 feet 11 inches wide, then the width of the cell itself was 4 feet and the only way to get into the bed was to crawl onto it from the foot. I suppose the bed was about 6 feet 6 inches long, and as it seemed to take up at least half of the cell, the whole was a sort of slot, roughly 12 feet by 4. As well as the bed there were two shelves, a small desk and a chair. The showers and lavatories were across the corridor.

To be fair, it was all perfectly clean, and there was a light over the bed so it was possible to read. Otherwise the policy of the management was obviously to keep their guests out of the hotel as much as possible by offering them no inducement to be in it. There was nothing by way of a sitting room, lounge, bar or television room, and the only general accommodation was a big room with formica-topped tables which opened up at breakfast time but was otherwise shut. Still, I was able to wash and dress and read and sleep, and I got a sort of wry amusement from having, at my advanced age, stumbled into this sparse and uncomfortable version of a youth hostel.

I dined that night on a green salad, a vast pizza and a huge glass of red wine, costing €12. This amounted, with the tip, to about £10 and was the first indication I had that in Germany, and later in Austria, things tended to be priced at the same number of euros as they would pounds in England. I would have been happy to pay £12 for that meal in England, but here I paid €12, which made it cheaper by nearly a third.

The month was September, and I came out next morning into bright sunshine. The admirable Lufthansa had treated my bicycle with such tender care that it was completely undamaged, but there was, as there always is, a problem. Somewhere along the way the connector had dropped out of the bicycle pump and gone missing, so I could not pump up the tyres, which had had to be half-deflated before the cycle was airborne. The hotel was at one end of Passau and they told me there was a bicycle shop almost at the other, so I paced the greater part of Passau, bought a new connector, walked all the way back to the hotel and in trying to pump up my tyres, broke the pump. Then I pushed the bicycle to the shop where the man pumped up the tyres with his pressure pump, and sold me a new pump for the journey, which did not work. At least it did not seem to work on my own particular bicycle but I only discovered this after I got home to England, as the pumping up administered in Passau lasted for the rest of the trip.

All of this walking to and fro was done beside the Danube, on which they have the most enormous barges. Several of these were moored by the bank and I paced out the length of one, which came to 110 good strides. It must have been about 100 metres long, which is an Olympic distance, and means, when you think about it, that men train for years and take illegal drugs in an effort to run the length of a Danube barge more quickly than the next man. This seems a strange thing to do when you think of it like that. These barges have engines and are steered from the rear, and to manoeuvre from the stern a boat of which the bow is an Olympic distance away must be a tricky business. I have a friend who took his family on holiday in a longboat on an English canal. When they came back I asked, as one does, 'How was the holiday?' It was, he said, 'the shortest route to a heart attack you could possibly imagine.' Longboats are trifling little things compared to Danube barges, and while I never met a Danube bargee, I am convinced that they are all men of strong constitutions and steady nerves.

My bicycle difficulty being solved, I was now free to wander about Passau, which I liked very much. It is at the confluence of three rivers, and this is a pleasant thing if only because it gives one the chance to use the word confluence, which I had never come across before and have never needed to use since. The three rivers are the Danube, the Inn and the Ilz, and what Dr Johnson might well have called the point of confluxion is to be found on a grassy tree-studded tongue of land where the Inn comes in from the right, with the Ilz appearing from the left. The hills over on the right bank are in Austria, but the border on the left bank is 24 kilometres away. Off to the left, at the mouth of the Ilz, you see a great fortress, or rather two fortresses called Veste Oberhaus and Veste Niederhaus, originating from the thirteenth century and now connected with a joining wall. The Inn has made its way from Switzerland, the Ilz from some forest in Bavaria, and they are now swallowed up by the Danube. The view from this point is impressive, with hills and woods above and the Danube striding off, as it were, in a purposeful manner towards the Black Sea.

Passau is a very good place for walking about, it being an old town (or at least that part of it they call the Old Town is an old town.) It was the seat of a series of Prince Bishops, which title was given to the then Bishop Ulrich by Emperor Frederick II in 1217. It signified that the people of Passau were to be ruled by whatever princely bishop was installed from that time on, such bishop being a prince of the Holy Roman Empire. This was not what the citizens wanted, as they coveted the status of a free imperial town, and there was more than one uprising, the last being put down with great slaughter in 1367. In spite of which Passau became extremely rich. It was at one time the largest bishopric in the Holy Roman Empire and its Prince Bishops and prosperous merchants have left their mark in the form, among other things, of a fine cathedral, a noble *Rathaus*, a splendid library and cobbled streets with rich looking houses.

The *Rathaus* stands back from the Danube with an open square in front. It is generally described as 'fourteenth century' which is a bit of a liberty as it actually consists of eight buildings joined together in the nineteenth century, while the tall tower which rises at one end is a neo-Gothic affair completed in 1892. The Great Fire of Passau of 1662, coming four years earlier than the Great Fire of London, did much damage to the original buildings, and more damage was done by the great floods of 1501 and 1954, but all is now in excellent shape. There are two fine Assembly Rooms, the Greater and the Lesser, with vaulted ceilings and intricate, heavily gilded, stucco work from the seventeenth century.

The Greater Assembly Room has allegorical and historical paintings on the ceilings, including, says the guidebook 'scenes from the *Nibelungenlied*'. 'Does it indeed?' you may say, possibly with rather a blank expression, which is how I reacted when I read the words. Since then I have found the story set out in the *Oxford Companion to English Literature*, which seems a strange place for a thirteenth-century German epic to be described, but so it is. The Nibelungs were, it seems, a race of dwarfs who lived in Norway. They had a hoard of treasure, guarded by a dwarf called Alberich, which passed into the hands of Siegfried and ended up in the Rhine guarded by Rhine Maidens. In spite of the efforts of the

Oxford Companion to explain it simply, the whole series of events and adventures is so complex that it left me reeling. Characters called Kreimhild, Gunther, Hagen, Brunhild and Etzel come and go, sometimes in Burgundy and sometimes in Iceland. The *Companion* does not say that the Danube was the scene of any of their exploits, but in one of the Assembly Rooms Kreimhild is shown arriving in Passau, where she was met by her uncle whose name is given simply as Bishop Pilgrim, so I take him to have been a mythological bishop much earlier than the Prince Bishops. Having encountered Kreimhild at Passau, I later came across odd references to *Nibelungenlied* characters at different places along the way. There is perhaps, even probably, nothing in all this that you do not already know if you are an opera buff, as these are the characters who figure in the *Ring* of Wagner.

The Lesser Assembly Room has a ceiling painting called the *Homage of the Three Rivers*, which shows the trio at the feet of Passavia, evidently a mythological or latinized and somehow more respectful name for Passau. Passavia is wearing a flowing golden dress; the Inn is represented by a wild-looking man clutching an uprooted tree while the Danube and the Ilz are goddesses wearing nothing much at all. The effect is luxurious and gorgeous and rich and ornate.

The bishops, at the beginning of the eighteenth century, built themselves a *Residenz* nearby, which has a staircase rising in a grand sweep of marble and stucco with a magnificent painted ceiling above. At the top I came upon a library with a rather surprised librarian from whom I got the impression that not many people knew that either she or it were there. It was a long vaulted room with *trompe l'œil* paintings, and handsome leather volumes which were just for show and not for study. There are two ways to stop people from getting a book in a library, one being to lock them in glass cases and the other to stretch wires along in front, which would have to be undone to get the books off the shelves. As far as I recall, at Passau they used the wire method. Although these books seemed mainly to be ornamental, the librarian herself was hard at work on some project of her own, and looked up in some astonishment when I appeared.

A stone's throw from the *Residenz* is St Stephen's Cathedral. In front of it is a statue of King Maximilian I Joseph of Bavaria, who has his hand held out in a way which suggests he has just stepped out to see if it has stopped raining. (This has not gone unnoticed by the people of Passau, who call him 'the rain-tester'.) The cathedral behind is very large, very white and very ornate. It is the work of an Italian architect and an Italian painter of the late-seventeenth century and is about as baroque as you can get. I admired the great central cupola from which God the Father looks down upon humanity below, but I have to confess that otherwise the words 'wedding cake' rose to my lips. I could see that the marble and stucco and gilding were very fine, but the whiteness of the building was too much like icing. The cathedral has, I am able to tell you, the biggest church organ in the whole wide world. It has 17,774 pipes and 233 stops, which is, I gather, a record. With great benevolence they give a free concert on the organ at noon every day and to fill in the time I went wandering round the market in the square beyond the rain-tester. As 12 approached I went back to the cathedral and as I mounted the steps the clock struck and at the first stroke the cathedral door was firmly shut in my face and as firmly locked. From 12 precisely those that are out are shut out and those that are in are shut in, for the next half hour. I can see that this is a good way to prevent disruption of the concert by tourists coming and going, but I just warn you that if you want to get in for the start of the concert, or get out between 12 and half past, you must look sharp about it.

In spite of this disappointment I was very pleased with Passau. There were plenty of visitors, very many of whom were wheeling bicycles about as if they had just arrived from somewhere else and had not yet found anywhere to park. I saw no organized and guided groups and it does not seem that Passau is on any Japanese tourist route as the wily oriental was only to be seen in rare glimpses, as opposed to the solid phalanxes which one encounters in better known places. There is a Museum of Modern Art which I took good care to avoid as I do not like the sort of stuff they have in places like that. Otherwise there seemed to be no great exhausting galleries which I might have felt obliged to queue up to get into. 'I like this,' said I to myself, 'much better than Florence.'

Now that is a ridiculous remark. If one imagines a debate and I were to propose the motion that 'this House considers Passau to be a better place than Florence', I should be smashed to smithereens by any halfway competent art historian on the other side. He need only extol the virtues of the Uffizi Gallery, the glories of Michelangelo's *David* and the charms of the Ponte Vecchio and I should be left looking silly. Still, I had that thought because we had recently been to Florence and come away without any wish to go again, whereas I would like to go back to Passau as I am sure there was more to be seen in the city itself and much more to be found in the country roundabout, than I discovered in the short time I was there. As for Florence, I will explain further.

The only thing wrong with our trip to Florence was Florence itself. Everything else was splendid, and it happened like this: We have a friend who was at the time a director of Saga. 'Would you like to come on a shakedown cruise?' she said.

'A shakedown cruise? Whatever is that?'

'We have a new ship coming out of dock and we are going to test it out.'

'To test it out? To see if it floats and the engines work?'

'No – no. To test the food and the plumbing.'

She explained that the shakedown cruise would last for two days, and as two days is about as long as I could stand being bottled up in a ship with a lot of other people, we accepted. The ship, she said, was called the *Spirit of Adventure*, which suggested that we might have to do something spirited and adventurous, such as allowing ourselves to be winched off the deck by a helicopter in a high sea, but she assured us that nothing of that sort could possibly be required.

She was right. Everything was as smooth as could be, including the ocean. A shakedown cruise is, we discovered, an excuse for a spree, an extended party given by the chief executive mainly for his friends, who seemed to be agreeably rich. Some people are disagreeably rich, but they were not, and being agreeably rich they were used to having the best of everything. When the chief executive gives a party for such people, the best of everything is what they get, and so did we. We had our first glass of champagne at Friday lunch time and our last at Sunday lunch time and two most memorable dinners in between.

Among the agreeably rich there was a sprinkling of the reasonably famous. The ship's captain, as by law required, organized a boat drill before we set off, and I enjoyed the sight of many well-known people struggling into orange lifejackets. I said to Anna Ford, the beautiful newsreader, that I thought hers became her and she ought to wear one more often. She thanked me politely but it was not really true. She looked pretty good in it but she looked much better without it, and as a fashion accessory it was not up to much. My wife spotted Dame Stella Rimington, the former head of MI5, and as my wife once worked for that mysterious organisation they tended to drift into conversation by themselves. I kept well out of earshot as I presumed they were reminiscing about the old spy-catching days and I did not wish to be party to a breach of the Official Secrets Act.

We flew to Nice, and the ship then took us by night from Nice to Livorno, and from there we went to Florence. We went ashore in Livorno, got in a bus and two hours later got off in Florence and started trooping along behind a guide. I had seen this sort of thing happening to other people. I had observed in different places cruise ships steaming into port like great mobile prison hulks. I had seen the imprisoned tourists marched ashore in gangs and lectured in broken English on the finer points of churches and monuments in which they were not much interested. I looked closely at the prisoners and could tell that their main wish was to get back to the ship and have a drink. That, more or less, is a description of us in Florence.

Tour guides, in my experience, seem always to fancy themselves as humorists and although their jokes are not usually good the tourists feel obliged to laugh out of politeness. There was a bit of that on the bus as a preliminary to the city itself. In Florence we changed to another guide who was rather small and from time to time went out of sight. It was bitterly cold, which caused John Cole, the former BBC political correspondent, to put on a bright red fleece and this was a help because whenever we lost the guide we could steer on John Cole and his fleece. We stared dutifully at a replica of Michelangelo's *David*, but did not attempt the rigours of the Uffizi Gallery. We crossed the Ponte Vecchio and then we crossed it back again. We looked respectfully at some statues in the Piazza della Signoria and we went into the Basilica di Santa Croce and found the tombs of Michelangelo and Galileo and the cenotaph of Dante. The guide then said we could now have some time to ourselves, so we had a sandwich and a glass of wine, looked at the shops and then went gratefully back to the bus.

The month was February and Florence was, to my eyes, dull and forbidding. I asked the guide which was the best time to come and she said, 'Now, because from spring to autumn it gets terribly crowded.' Well, if I was seeing Florence at its best, I should not like to see it at its worst, whereas I felt that Passau was an easy-going sort of place that would be pleasant at any time. This is why I preferred it, but the idea is, as I have said, aesthetically indefensible.

So, on the morning of my second day in Passau I scrambled over the foot of my bed, extricated myself from my cell, removed my bicycle from the cage, and set off. Getting out of Passau on the right road is the easiest thing in the world. You ride towards the point where the three rivers meet, turn left across the Danube by the suspension bridge, turn right to cross the Ilz on another bridge and you are now on the Donauradweg. This may be a formidable looking word to those who have even less German than I, and it may help if I say that you pronounce it Don-ow-rard-vegg; it means the Danube cycle track and it takes you to Vienna.

The cycle track is supposed to be marked throughout with green and white signs and, unlike the Romantische Strasse, it almost always is, though occasionally you are tipped out onto a road and left to assume that you are on the right path. There are plenty of cyclists scattered about so you can usually find one to follow if in doubt, and anyway the Danube itself is the best guide because it is generally there, clearly visible at your side. The Radweg out of Passau starts off beside a busy road and is at this stage neither inspiriting nor encouraging. From time to time traffic is siphoned off by subsidiary roads to the left, so the one you are following gets gradually quieter. After a bit of this, the main road disappears altogether leaving you on a very quiet road indeed, which then becomes the simplest of farm roads, just like those of the Romantische Strasse except that instead of fields on both sides you have fields to the left and the Danube to the right. You now feel yourself to be off and away, and the spirits lift.

The Danube is very lovely, but is it blue? It is generally greeny-brown, which is usual with rivers that have silt at the bottom and trees at the side. However, to do it justice, if you catch it at the right angle under a clear blue sky it can, with a touch of imagination, be taken as blue. This could possibly be true of many rivers, but in the case of the Danube one looks out for the blue effect and, in fine September weather, one gets it quite often.

I had my passport at the ready in the pocket of my shirt because I knew that before long I would come to the Austrian border. My idea of a proper continental border is a fence patrolled by men with Alsatian dogs. At any crossing point there should be a barrier which can be raised, like the gate of a level crossing. There ought to be sentry boxes with men in khaki or possibly blue, some with pistols at their side and others nursing machine guns. Anyone passing through is to be regarded with suspicion, and in these days of high technology, some check made to see if they are wanted for any special crime or on any general suspicion of being terrorists. In terms of such activity the Austrian border was a disappointment. There was no fence, no dogs, no barrier, not a soldier to be seen and my passport stayed in my pocket. The border between Germany and Austria comes in the form of a little bridge over a little stream in the middle of farmland, with a little dilapidated notice telling you that once past this sign you are in Austria. I would have missed it altogether if another cyclist had not pointed it out.

I was particularly glad to be in Austria because of a man called Jörg Haider, whom the Austrian people some years before had chosen to be their leader. I do not think he ever did anything very terrible or ever said anything too outrageous, but he was definitely a very right-wing politician. The bigwigs of the European Union took offence at the idea that the Austrian nation should, by fair and open democratic process, elect such a man to high office. They said they would not shake hands with him, and began to huff and puff, and vaguely to mutter about some collective punishment – but then couldn't think of one, and dropped the idea altogether. The European Union is, as one knows, a corrupt, inefficient and inter-meddling institution, and the notion that the Austrian people might only vote for politicians capable of passing some test of moral purity devised in Brussels was, I thought, yet another step too far (most steps taken by Brussels being of this nature). I felt at the time that I ought to mount a counter-demonstration in favour of Austrian democracy by going there at once and cycling down the Danube to show my support. For whatever reason I couldn't or didn't do it then, and by now Jörg Haider seemed to have vanished, but still I felt that I was, at last and belatedly, fulfilling a previous obligation.

In passing from Germany to Austria one passes, according to my theory, from *Morgen* and *Abend* country into *Grüss Gott* country. By this I mean that the usual form of greeting changes. In Germany they seem to say '*Guten Morgen* – good morning' and '*Guten Abend* – good evening', sometimes, like us, dropping the *guten* bit and just saying '*Morgen*' or '*Abend*'. In Austria they greet you with '*Grüss Gott*' which sounds a bit like 'Great Scot' and means – exactly what I am not sure. '*Grüss*' means 'greet' and '*Gott*' means 'God' but I cannot be sure of the exact significance of the two together. I have asked the best German scholar I know and he says it is just a sort of formula, like 'How do you do?' which was once an enquiry after the other person's health, but is no longer.

The cycling was, by now, superb, aided by a phenomenon which I will here introduce as the Loch Lomond Effect. On the only occasion that my wife and I drove to the Highlands of Scotland we noticed that on the banks of Loch Lomond the road, which was perhaps about 8 feet above the loch, seemed to slope gently downwards but never got any closer to the water. It was a mystery. Obviously the surface of the loch was lively and it might be ruffled but it is manifestly impossible that it should slope in parallel with the road. Equally obviously the road appeared most certainly to be on a gentle decline, and it was just as manifestly impossible that it should go continually downwards without ever reaching the level of the water. This, I can only assume, must be some sort of an optical illusion. In just the same way, cycling by the Danube, which is anyway easy because the Radweg is flat, is made even easier by the Loch Lomond Effect, as in an obliging way the Radweg makes you feel that you are going downhill without taking you splash into the Danube.

This, at least, is what happens if you are going downstream, and of course the important question occurred to me: 'Does it work in the other direction?' I was going from Passau to Vienna because the lady in Greece told me to. Had she told me to go from Vienna to Passau I would have done it that way, and I know of no reason why you shouldn't do it in that direction if you felt like it. However, to see whether you would then get the great benefit of the Loch Lomond Effect, I turned round and started cycling upstream, and seemed to be going neither uphill nor downhill but simply on the flat. I did not go very far in the wrong direction, and perhaps the effect would have become apparent if I had persevered, but my tentative conclusion, which others may like to put to the test, is that the Loch Lomond Effect only operates downstream.

Downhill or not, the Danube is an admirable river to cycle beside. It is very wide – I guessed about 300 metres. It is very fast flowing and in this early part it often funnels its way between very steep banks. On your land side you may then be shut in by big trees, so that what you see is what is on the other side – houses, villages, patches of farmland, churches, hills and more trees. Sometimes the banks rise so abruptly that, apart from the Radweg, there is no room for anything on either side except trees. The Danube is also a busy river – a working river, and a hard-working river at that because there are 100-metre barges going up and down all the time, with occasional speedboats and now and then a passenger boat. On the cycle track there was a sparse but steady flow of people doing the same as I. In September at least it is not crowded, but you have to keep a sharp ear open if you are dawdling along as I was, in case some speedier cyclist wants to shoot past you from behind.

My intention was to stay at *Gasthofs*, or rather *Gasthöfe*, in preference to hotels because I liked the word better. A *Gasthof* sounds an altogether more Austrian kind of thing than a hotel, and I spell it like that because in German they like to give capital letters to all their common nouns. Sometimes the word appears as *Gasthaus*, and as far as I can make out that means much the same thing, *Gasthof* and *Gasthaus* being interchangeable words, but *Gasthof* perhaps suggesting a slightly grander establishment. I stopped for coffee at a most promising *Gasthof* overlooking the river where I would very much have liked to stay, but it came a bit too soon. I had planned to stay at a place called Schlögen which was, said the waitress, 8 kilometres further on so on I went.

At Schlögen you are obliged to cross the river. I had not known this, though it is a bit of information that might have been buried somewhere among the German package tour brochure that I had acquired. There was no obvious reason why one should cross. The cycle path seemed to go on ahead, but there was a little ferryboat with a ferryman who said that the track ran out after 600 metres and the only way to make further progress was to cross to the other side on his ferry. Such at least is my interpretation of his high speed German, although I thought at the time that it might just have been sales talk to drum up business for his ferry. However, it convinced some other cyclists who now arrived. Each of them handed him €2 and piled into his ferry, so I gave him the same and piled in as well. I later discovered that, at least in September, the ferryman knocks off at 6 p.m., and that evening I saw some unfortunates apparently stranded on the other side, gazing disconsolately across, rather as if the Danube was the Styx and they were dead, and longing to get back to life. Their remedy must have been to cycle 8 kilometres back to the Gasthof where I had had coffee, and I expect that that establishment gets a certain amount of business by way of fallout by people who mean to stay in Schlögen but are frustrated by this latter-day Charon.

Schlögen is not a place, it is a spot on the map. By this I mean there is no visible village, but there are places to stay. The German package-tour brochure had a picture of a promising-looking place, and there it was, on the far side, painted a particularly hideous shade of yellow, a colour which seems to be popular in these parts. It was called the Hotel Donauschlinge and I booked in, somewhat intimidated to find that it was a four-star establishment. I had not meant to stay in effeminate luxury and at €69 it was, by my standards, expensive. However, I added the cost of bed and breakfast there to the cost of my two nights in Passau, divided the total by three and found my average expenditure to be about £30 a night which was a more cheerful way to look at it.

I had a lovely big room with huge windows looking over the river and it was worth the money to revel in spacious elegance after the cramped conditions of the two nights before. Also, in terms of euros per square metre the Schlögen room was much better value than my cell at Passau, as I could have fitted eight or ten of the latter into the former. While I have no regrets, for the sake of those who come after me I will say that I later found at Schlögen a humbler *Gasthof* of an even more hideous yellow which can be reached by climbing about a hundred metres up a small hill in the upstream direction. There are also signs saying that if you cycle a further 4 kilometres towards Linz you will find two more *Gasthöfe*. However, the situation at Schlögen is so superb that I recommend you not to go on but to stay there, either at the *Gasthof* or the Donauschlinge. If you choose the Donauschlinge, bring your swimming things as there is a tempting indoor pool which was no good to me as I had no trunks and did not dare to swim in my underpants.

The great point about Schlögen is that the river here comes bang up against an impenetrable wall of mountain and as it cannot go back the way it came it is obliged to loop off in a hairpin bend called the Schlögener Schlinge. The word *Schlinge* is, as you may have guessed, the German for loop, so that the Hotel Donauschlinge is the Danube Loop Hotel. Trees come right down to the water's edge, with Schlögen itself built at the top of the bend, and it is very, very beautiful. There is a wide bay with a cluster of small boats, from which three speedboats came out and put on a performance of chasing each other round the great sweep of water in front of the hotel. I thought at first that they were like playful dolphins, but then decided they were more like predatory sharks and rather hoped they would crash into each other and so provide some extra excitement for the spectators, but they didn't. Having watched them for a bit I climbed up into the woods, which is something you are encouraged to do because there is a well-marked path. From high up I found a gap in the trees through which I was able to survey with considerable satisfaction a wide view of the great river as it performed its spectacular volte-face below.

What with this walk, and the cycle ride of about 65 kilometres, I went into the hotel dining room with a hearty appetite and high expectations. I settled myself at a corner table, took up my book and was immediately evicted. I do not know why this happened, as I was perfectly properly dressed. She who was, I suppose, the head waitress, insisted that I be shuffled off down a corridor to a side table away from the main action where I was, for a time, forgotten. Eventually the thought came to this same woman that I might want something to eat and so, in a grudging way, she took my order. I asked for medallions of pork, which I knew from past experience can be delicious, but these I think had been cooked some weeks before and given a quick re-heat in the microwave. They did not cost much and therefore were in some sense like my room in Passau – cheap but a bit grim.

This is a comment which, with some regret, I have to say applies quite widely to Austrian food. I have a particular aversion to Wiener schnitzel, and any nation that favours that concoction of greasy batter must have something funny about it. I took good care not to have any schnitzels on this trip, and the Austrian food that I ate after this was always all right but never exciting. The admirable solution to the problem of public eating that has been arrived at over recent years in many parts of the world is the great proliferation of Italian restaurants. Almost everywhere there are now Italian restaurants and they always seem to be good. We have found it quite easy to get a poor meal in France, for all their swanking about their food, and the way to be certain of a good meal in France is to go to an Italian restaurant. As there are Italian restaurants all over Austria as well as all over everywhere else, those were the places where, when possible, I ate.

I parted from the Hotel Donauschlinge with mixed feelings. Schlögen is the obvious place to spend the first night for those who have set off from Passau, and being in a near monopoly position the Donauschlinge is able to relieve its customers of their money without putting itself to much trouble. I do not think anyone stays for any length of time, and as we were just passing through and not likely to come again there was no need for the hotel staff to bother much about us. The place itself is enormous, and swarms with cyclists, some of whom I suspect are of the inferior variety who have their luggage transported for them in vans or lorries. All these things are against it. On the other hand, for an honest traveller who carries his bags with him, like me, it does provide rooms of great comfort and luxury in a splendid situation, and this is definitely in its favour. One cannot, after all, have everything.

After an hour or so of pedalling towards Linz that morning I stopped to rest by the Danube. Trees, bright sunshine and blue skies made the river green in front of me but decidedly blue in mid-stream over to the left. I sat relishing the silence broken only by the gentle lapping of the river against a little rocky causeway which someone at some time must have built

ng purpose. There was no possibility of traffic
w metalled road beside the water, unless you
ts, and at 10.20 on this Sunday morning there
were no many of them.

For a long way after Schlögen the banks of the river are
almost uninhabited. I passed the two benevolent *Gasthaus*-
cum-restaurant establishments which had been predicted
by the sign at Schlögen, and there were a couple of little
settlements to be seen on the other side, but otherwise there
is just forest coming down steep slopes right to the water's
edge. At Neuhaus there was a small ramshackle cafe grandly
named the Kaiserhof where I stopped and asked for tea.
There being many peculiar herbal teas now available they
demanded to know what sort of tea I wanted and rattled
off a whole lot of words that probably meant camomile
or blackcurrant and things like that. In England the words
'builders' tea' produce the sort of brew that I am after and
here I discovered that the words *'Schwarze Tee'* – black tea
– bring on the nearest approximation to the right stuff one
can get in Austria. It comes in the form of a Tetley's tea bag
and some hot water.

I say that I was at Neuhaus when I discovered all this because
there was a sign on the bank with that name on it but there
was no village that I could see – only the Kaiserhof. Across
the river there was a castle called, according to my brochure,
Schloss Neuhaus. This castle, which looked down upon us

from a great height, was obviously just as much in Neuhaus as the Kaiserhof cafe, but I could not see how you could have a Neuhaus on both the left and right banks of the Danube unless the two parts were connected by a bridge, which they were not. I cannot find a mention of Neuhaus in any modern guidebook, but Baedeker of 1900 tells us that there is 'at Neuhaus a handsome chateau on a lofty wooded height, the property of Herr von Plank'. I could see that Herr von Plank had lived in pretty good style, so perhaps he had property on both sides of the river, an Upper Neuhaus for superior persons such as himself and a Lower Neuhaus for the lower classes down where I was.

After Neuhaus comes Aschach, which provided my first encounter with one of the small and attractive towns that lie beside the Danube. It stretches along the river with a collection of very pretty, highly decorated houses, painted pink, blue or yellow, and I rode up and down the town admiring them. Aschach is on both sides of the river but, unlike Neuhaus, both parts are connected by a bridge. The Danube had by now widened out, and being curious to know how wide it was, I paced it out and that part of the bridge which was directly over the water came to 280 paces, which I found a little disappointing, as I would have guessed that it was more.

Then, in the sunshine by the river, I had an Austrian lunch consisting of beer, bread, three frankfurters and mustard.

The food all came on one plate but there was no knife or fork. I waited to see if such things would arrive, but they did not, so I looked rather furtively round to see how others were managing, and saw that the proper thing to do is to grasp one end of a frankfurter, dip the other end in the mustard and eat it in your fingers. As I like frankfurters and like mustard, this was a pretty good lunch.

There is, as everyone knows, an everlasting argument between us old people and the younger generation. We say things were much better when we were young, and they say we only say that because we are old and old people always talk like that. In this dispute I have come to realize that we old ones have a card in our hand which they can never hold, because they are saying what they think, but we are talking about what we know. We were there, and they were not. Now as an example, not of my youth but of my father's youth, and of the way things have gone off between then and now, I will tell you that if you arrived with the current Baedeker in your luggage, and looked up the entry for Aschach, you would find this: 'At the straggling little town of Aschach (267m–876ft) with a row of 16th–18th c. gabled houses, the hills draw away from the river and open up a view of the chain of the Alps. A bridge crosses the Danube near Aschach', and that is all he has to say. By contrast, Baedeker of 1900, after enthusing about the view of the Styrian and Austrian Alps, says this: 'From this point to Linz and beyond it, the valley was the scene of many sanguinary encounters during the revolt of the peasantry of Upper Austria. In 1626 Aschach was the headquarters of the insurgents, where, as well as at Neuhaus, they had barricaded the Danube with chains to prevent the Bavarians from assisting Count Herberstein, the Austrian governor, who was shut up at Linz.' I think that if one is passing through scenes of sanguinary encounters with insurgent peasantry, writers of guidebooks should certainly mention the matter and Baedeker of 1900 was quite right to do so. It gives the imagination something to work on as you cycle along, and it would have been even more helpful if Baedeker, old or new, had explained that the insurgent peasants were Protestants in revolt against the efforts of Maximilian of Bavaria to turn them into Catholics.

After Aschach the riverbank widens out and there is sometimes a road beside the Radweg, and for some of the time there is what looks like a disused canal. In order to follow the Radweg you must cross the left bank at Ottensheim, which you do on a ferry. In this case it is a proper professional ferry capable of taking motorcars, rather than the tiny little boat that plies to and fro at Schlögen. My plan was to sleep that night at Linz, but if I were to do it again I would stay at Ottensheim. This is partly because Linz is a very large place while Ottensheim is a small one, and I prefer small places to large, and also because Ottensheim makes a very good impression as you approach by ferry. This is confirmed when you go ashore. There are grassy banks, rising to a terrace of fine houses, with the church spire behind. If you climb up to the centre of things you find a spacious and elegant square in which people were sitting around drinking coffee in a leisurely continental manner. It is one of those places which has an agreeable atmosphere, and as there was more than one place to stay, my advice to anyone passing this way is to do so, but I did not, and rode on for Linz as Linz was in my plan.

Six kilometres outside Linz the left pedal came off my bicycle. It had shown signs of being loose earlier in the day and I had tightened it twice. Now it sagged at a feeble angle and when I took a hold of it, came away in my hand like a loose tooth. This bicycle, which had served me well in different countries must, I supposed, be feeling its age. For some animals, such as dogs, to get an idea of how old they are in human terms you multiply their actual years by seven. If a dog is three years old, this is thought to be equivalent to twenty-one for one of us. Applying this to bicycles, then mine was the same age as me. I had had it for eleven years so it and I were both, humanly speaking, seventy-seven. That it should be suffering from a certain amount of wear and tear was something I could understand and with which I could sympathize. Also, to give it due credit, if it was to shed a pedal, then a spot 6 kilometres outside Linz was a reasonable place to do it. If it had done it at the start of the day at Schlögen I should have been miles from a mechanic, but as Linz is a big industrial city I was, presumably, within 6 kilometres or so of help.

I now established, beyond all doubt, that unless you are some kind of a trick cyclist you cannot ride a bicycle with only one pedal. I tried it, and it did not work. I got on, pushed down on the right pedal and down it stayed, there being no means of bringing it up. Possibly if I had toe caps on my pedals I might have been able somehow to pull it up, but I hadn't and so couldn't. The first expedient I tried was to find, with some difficulty, a stick which would fit into the hole left by the missing pedal. I found one, shoved it in, got on, trod hard on the right pedal, pressed gently on the stick and it immediately snapped. Then I tried putting the loose pedal back into the hole and by pushing inwards as well as downwards managed to keep it precariously in place for a few short bursts. By this means the bicycle and I limped along for two more kilometres after which the pedal fell out altogether and absolutely refused to play any further part in my progress, so I made an inglorious entry into Linz on foot and pushing the bicycle.

The cycle track into Linz is not pleasant as there is a busy road beside it. Linz gets a favourable mention in guidebooks but only, I think, because it is a great big place and they cannot ignore it altogether. If I were going again I should certainly ignore it, unless I happened to have an ailing bicycle needing attention. It is a huge manufacturing town, and for cycling purposes the best way to treat it would be to ride straight through it, having stayed, as suggested, at Ottensheim, and heading for the next place, which is Mauthausen.

As it was, having got near to the bridge which crosses the river from the new town to the old, I asked a helpful passer-by to tell me how to find a hotel, and he directed me onto the main road which leads directly away from the bridge. On the right hand side I came to a hotel where a pretty Chinese receptionist told me I could have a room for €180 but that there was a cheaper place further on. I thanked her for this useful information and pushed my loaded bicycle laboriously along until I reached the Goldener Adler, where I got a room for €60. To anyone who persists in staying in Linz in spite of my advice against it, I recommend the Goldener Adler. I found that it is a recognized cyclists' stopping point as there were a great many bicycles in the yard and some obvious cyclists in the breakfast room next day. To make absolutely plain the way to find it, I will tell you that you should get on the right hand side of the road that comes directly from the bridge, with the Danube behind you, and it is the second hotel that you come to. I say all this because Linz can be a puzzling place and easy to get lost in, especially if you arrive late. I know this because I later encountered a distraught middle aged Austro-German lady with a bicycle who flapped her guidebook at me and asked in near panic if I had any idea how to find the hotel recommended in it. As the hotel in question was not the Goldener Adler I was, alas, unable to help, but I suggested that she abandon that hotel and go to the Goldener Adler instead, this being the most calming thing that I could think of. As I never saw her again I expect she found the one she wanted or else got lost altogether.

There being nothing to be done about the pedal that evening I walked across the bridge to have a look at the old town of Linz and came into a handsome square with trams running through it. In the centre was a column that started from a rectangular base, became curly like a snake, and supported two figures in bright gold with a sort of golden sun above, having golden rays shooting out all round. The two figures and the sun represent the Trinity, and this is the Trinity Column which was put up in 1723 in thanks for deliverance from fire, plague and the Turks. I cannot explain the fire and plague, except that they were common occurrences at the time, but Turks are a different matter. After the fall of Constantinople in 1483 the Ottoman Turks gradually pushed westwards until their empire extended over Hungary. Then, in a sudden attack in 1683, they reached the gates of Vienna with an army of 200,000 men. They were there defeated by a combined Austrian, Polish and German army, and driven back in stages until the capture of Belgrade in 1718 put an end to the Turkish threat to Europe. Linz was pretty close to the front line and provided a refuge for Leopold I when Vienna was under siege. The Trinity Column was an expression of public gratitude for their narrow escape.

By wandering about I found a white baroque church which no doubt had its finer aspects, but I was tired beyond the point of appreciating them so I went back to the square and ordered a glass of white wine. Wine in Austria always seems to come by the glass, and I never saw anyone with a bottle of it, but I suppose such a thing can be got. The amount you get when you ask for a glass of wine seems to depend on the whim of the waiter or, in this case, the waitress. If you are in luck you get a *Viertel*, which is a quarter of a litre, but otherwise you get an *Achtel*, or half that amount. This time the girl thought my needs would be met with an *Achtel*, though I could have done with a *Viertel*. After that I found an Italian restaurant, ate too much, and fell quietly asleep at the Goldener Adler.

Linz-lovers throughout the world, and there may be many, will be shocked at the cursory and slighting way in which I have dismissed their city. This may perhaps be due to the mental fatigue which struck me at the end of the day, much as metal fatigue had afflicted my bicycle earlier. All the same, the trouble with Linz is that it is much too big, being the biggest city in Austria after Vienna and Graz. The guidebook says there are iron and steelworks and chemical factories, and I quite believe it. Still, I had found the old town and seen the *Hauptplatz*, the main square, which is said to be the important bit.

Next morning the helpful hotel clerk directed me to a cycle mechanic. The place was, he said sadly, 2 kilometres away and I wondered whether in such a bustling place as Linz there might not be one closer, bearing in mind that the whole Austrian nation is obsessed with the bicycle. There are cyclists everywhere; there are cycle racks everywhere; there are cycle tracks almost everywhere and where there is no cycle track it is quite the done thing to ride on the pavement. The lights at the pedestrian crossings have a little green man as in England, and a little green bicycle as well. The Dutch are generally thought to be the most devoted cyclists in Europe, and there may possibly be more bicycles per head of population in Holland than here, but the Austrians must run them a close second.

Anyway, it was not for me to argue with the man at the Goldener Adler, who must have advised many cyclists in his time, so I set off, pushing my poor lame bicycle along a series of busy roads and following the map that he had given me. After what seemed to be a good 2 kilometres I came to a huge and magnificent cycle emporium. There were gleaming bicycles and shining bits of bicycle all over the floor and hanging upon the walls, all of it under the care of a middle-aged man in a clean shirt and jeans, who was assisted by a young man in even cleaner shirt and even cleaner jeans. Neither of them looked like a mechanic and the whole place sparkled with cleanliness.

The young man looked at my bicycle and pronounced that the trouble was not in the pedal but in the shank into which it had to fit. The thread, he said, was worn.

Could I have a new shank?

On this point he would have to consult the middle-aged man. He of middle age was busy selling a new bicycle to a tricky customer whose plan seemed to be to try every model in the shop before he made up his mind, so some time passed before my request could be attended to. In due course the head man declared that I might have a new shank, took one out of a drawer and handed it to the young man, who fitted it without even getting his fingers dirty, let alone a spot of oil upon his immaculate jeans.

The bicycle being thus repaired, at a cost of about £20, I rode back on a combination of cycle tracks and pavements to the Goldener Adler. There I collected my panniers and set off for Mauthausen, but before I quit Linz altogether I should say that if things had turned out differently between 1939 and 1945 Linz might now be claiming some distinction from having provided Adolf Hitler with his secondary education, such as it was. Hitler was Austrian by birth and his father, a customs officer, wanted his son to follow him into the civil service and therefore enrolled him in the high school at Linz. Hitler, however, aspired to be a painter and so, according to himself, rebelled and did no work. He achieved academic failure and hated his teachers.

'I have,' he said later, 'the most unpleasant recollections of the teachers who taught me. Their external appearance exuded uncleanliness; their collars were unkempt... They were the product of a proletariat denuded of all personal independence of thought, distinguished by unparalleled ignorance.' In spite of these disagreeable recollections, when Germany seized control of Austria in 1938, Hitler paused in his triumphal progress to Vienna to tell the cheering crowds of Linz that: 'If Providence once called me forth from this town to be the leader of the Reich, it must in so doing have charged me with a mission, and that mission could only be to restore my dear homeland to the German Reich. I have believed in this mission, I have lived and fought for it, and I believe I have now fulfilled it.' I should imagine that these are all matters that the people of Linz would now prefer to forget.

The ride out of Linz is hardly more attractive than the entry into it, with factories and a huge coal-fired power station, or something similar, on the far bank. On your side of the river you pass through a pleasant park, and once you are out of that the country is flat or flattish, without the magnificent woods that have gone before. Also there comes a point where, although there appears to be a perfectly good cycle track ahead, a notice sternly commands you to leave the river and take to the road if you want to continue on the Donauradweg.

A mile or so before Mauthausen I stopped at a cafe where a yellow dog came out and sniffed at me. He was an Alsatian, but small for that breed, and an exact replica of a dog called Rolf who had belonged to me when I was in the army. The officers' mess of the 8th Hussars had a good many dogs in it, and Rolf was at the bottom of the heap, an underdog of underdogs or, if the phrase exists in German, *ein Unterhund von Unterhunden*. His trouble was psychological. He had belonged to a national service medical officer, and when the MO was demobilized he gave Rolf to another officer and departed. Alsatians are devoted one-man dogs and Rolf was so demoralized at this parting that he could not take to his new owner and degenerated into a sort of miserable cur. The other dogs bullied him, the officers spurned him and his second owner was ashamed of him. There were only two people who liked him; one was a German mess waiter called Heinz, and I was the other. I think that Heinz was sympathetic to Rolf because he himself was a bit of an underdog. He was a man of middle age but had to put up with being ordered about and occasionally shouted at by 8th Hussars officers, some of whom were scrubby boys hardly a year out of school. Whatever the reason for his sympathy, Heinz used to speak kindly to Rolf in German, and slip him scraps of food to cheer him up. I, on the other hand, admired Rolf for a trick which he had developed as a means of getting his revenge upon the bullies among the other dogs. You entered or left the mess by a swing door, and Rolf used to lie in wait until he saw one of his enemies approaching this door, and then, when that dog was halfway through, he would rush up and bite its bottom. To get his revenge the other dog had to go right through the swing door, turn round and come back again, by which time Rolf had gone. He always made sure of his escape route and could be seen flying across the lawn on his way to the stables or some other place of refuge. I was impressed by that, and having a general predilection for the underdog I asked if I could have him, and so Rolf became mine.

The top dog in the mess was a sleek black Labrador called Brumas, and one of Brumas's accomplishments was that he could jump. Outside the mess there was a wooden fence perhaps about 3 feet 6 inches high, and Brumas's owner would sometimes show off his dog's great ability by getting him to jump over it. I knew from my general knowledge that Alsatians also are often good jumpers, and I thought that perhaps if Rolf learned to jump, that might put him onto something nearer to an equal footing with Brumas. So, in the privacy of my room, I rigged up a very low jump made of a long stick between the end of the bed and the wastepaper basket. I managed to get it across to Rolf that when I jumped over this and said 'Over!' he was to follow me, and pretty soon he would jump it if I just said 'Over!' and didn't jump it myself. Of course, I lavished praise and encouragement upon him, which he liked. Little by little and over time I raised the obstacle till he could jump a pretty good height. Then I made a very narrow jump by putting my riding whip between two chairs and Rolf leapt over that without demur. After that, if we were outside, I could hold out my whip at arm's length and Rolf would jump over it. Then I found that I could take off my hat, hold it out and say 'Over!' and Rolf would jump over my hat.

This caused something of a sensation. No other officer of the 8th Hussars had a dog which would jump over his hat. Furthermore, I met Brumas and his owner outside the mess one day, and when Brumas was sent over the 3 feet 6 inches fence I pointed at it, said 'Over!' and Rolf flew over it in capital style, greatly impressing a number of onlookers.

The effect of all this was spectacular. Rolf no longer came slinking sheepishly into the mess but trotted in with head and tail held high. The other dogs did not bully him, and he did not bite their bottoms. My brother officers treated him kindly, and Heinz was delighted to see him in such good shape. But alas! It all ended in tragedy. When I too was demobilized I passed him on to a regular officer in the hope that continual jumping practice would see Rolf through this further change, but it did not work. I heard later that he had gone mad, not from rabies but from some sort of canine schizophrenia which made him unmanageable, and he had to be put down. Anyway, I now stroked the cafe owner's dog and told him he reminded me of Rolf, but I was a disappointment to him, because I gave him nothing to eat.

The road into Mauthausen took me through some uninteresting houses with an uninteresting *Gasthof* or two, and this was new Mauthausen. By following the little green signs I came, quite suddenly and much to my relief, to old Mauthausen, where I was reunited with the Danube. Here I stayed at the first self-declared *Gasthof* of the trip, everything else having been a hotel. A plump and motherly woman appeared to be delighted to see me, took me in and gave me a single room for €45 including breakfast. The room was once more a cell, but a nice cell, at least four times the size of the cell at Passau. Once settled in I had my lunch, which came in the form of two astonishingly long frankfurters with a bowl of French mustard and what looked like a pile of minced cabbage. It was all to be eaten with the fingers as before, and the minced cabbage was the hottest thing I have had in years. I have no idea what they spice it with, but it pretty well cauterizes the palate, excoriates the back of the nose and brings water freely to the eyes. That sounds like a complaint but it isn't, as I like hot food. Those who do not should be on their guard.

Old Mauthausen reeks of money, partly from having once been a customs port and partly from having dealt in salt. There is a barn of great antiquity built for the storage of salt and while salt has now become a disreputable commodity which wicked multinational companies put into potato crisps in order to make children fat, in its respectable days it helped make the people of Mauthausen rich. They used their money wisely from the Middle Ages onwards because they built themselves handsome houses. These are large, flat fronted, in perfect condition and painted every conceivable colour, including several shades of yellow and a surprising lime green. At the centre of the town there is:

A blue apothecary
An orange house next to the apothecary
A pink house next to the orange house
A bright yellow house next to the pink house
A lime green town hall
An off-pink public notary
A banana yellow primary school

As set down by me, the colour scheme may sound bizarre but as seen with the eye, it is bright and attractive.

I made my way up to the fourteenth-century Gothic church where there are some faint but sufficiently visible wall paintings and some startling combinations of black and gold by way of picture frames and pulpit. There are two beautiful modern stained glass windows and a modern altar which is not beautiful but looks as if it had been bought in a hurry from Ikea in order to bring the altar to the people as required by the Vatican. Very far from Ikea-ware were the noble old oak pews, designed with a view to the discomfort of the congregation. Each has a narrow seat and a projecting rail which sticks into your back when you sit down and would keep the most somnolent parishioner awake throughout the longest of sermons.

As well as its striking houses, Mauthausen has a museum. It is housed in a minor castle called Schloss Pragstein. Of all the museums in the world this must be the one of which they are most reluctant to let you see the contents. They only open it from 5 to 7 p.m., and that only on Tuesdays and Thursdays, and that only from May to October. From the leaflet which they give you to tell you what it is that you may not see, I got the impression that it was a fairly motley collection of local stuff such as farm implements and costume, so I was not too sorry to have missed one of the rare occasions when the doors are opened.

As well as the impenetrable museum there is a former concentration camp 5 kilometres from Mauthausen, and this you can visit if you want to. It was mainly a forced labour camp to provide workers in the nearby quarries but as half of the 200,000 people sent there were either worked to death or deliberately killed, it was as evil as you would expect any Nazi camp to be. Among those sent there for execution were a number of Russian, Polish, English, American and Dutch prisoners of war. I was in two minds as to whether I should go there. On the one hand I shrink from all horrors and tortures, and will not go to see a film about the navy in the days of sail as I know some unfortunate fellow will be flogged. Also I have a lingering doubt about the dangers of offering a concentration camp as something close to a tourist attraction. On the other hand I accept that there is a duty on us to accept and face such places at Mauthausen as giving a salutary lesson in the frightful barbarity of which mankind is readily capable. I chose the weaker course and did not go there, for which I have no better excuse than that I did not want to, and told myself that I was on holiday.

Mauthausen itself was an enjoyable place to wander about, but the view across the Danube is not altogether pleasant as there is a big crane and some sort of factory-like building on the other side. Nor are the outskirts of Mauthausen pleasant, as I found when I cycled off next day. On the left is a strung-out succession of builders' yards and storage sheds and other buildings of that sort. Then you emerge onto a proper Radweg with trees on the far side of the river and shrubs on yours, and things look up. There is, I noticed, remarkably little wildlife by the Danube. A bunch of swans, a couple of ducks and a heron were all that I had seen on the river so far. It being September, not much was to be expected by way of birdsong, but as there were no visible birds on the bank beyond a couple of crows, I don't suppose there is birdsong in spring. There were, though, a number of rollerbladers, which sounds like some sort of bird but is actually a person on wheels.

Austrians in these parts are keen on rollerblading, and may be like the Canadians in the colder parts of Canada who skate on ice all winter and rollerblade all summer. Austrians like to rollerblade along the Donauradweg and they go at a fair speed – a bit slower than me on my bicycle, but not much. There are also a number of walkers, some of whom go in for that form of walking which involves punting yourself along with two long rubber-tipped ski sticks, which I suspect is just an idea that someone thought up to increase the sale of ski sticks. Once, and only once, I saw a man who had combined the two, and was rollerblading along with ski sticks. I can imagine that this might possibly be effective, as if you are on wheels, punting along with ski sticks may be more of a help than a hindrance. There might even be scope here for someone to get into the *Guinness World Records* by rollerblading beside the Danube from Passau to the Black Sea, in the hope that this is further than anyone has rollerbladed before. If any keen rollerblader should read these pages and be tempted to rollerblade, if not to the Black Sea at least from Passau to Vienna, I can see only one difficulty, which I will come to in its proper place. The difficulty is, I think, superable, which is the sort of word one of my tutors at Oxford was keen on using.

The Radweg was now empty, and I rode happily along without seeing anybody else for about an hour and a quarter. After that I reached a welcome oasis in the form of a kiosk which had a tap with running water and was selling coffee. There were a few other people either filling their water bottles at the one or recruiting their strength with the other, and I did both. Then there was an excellent spell of cycling, leaving the Danube for a time and weaving through wide open farmland with prosperous farmhouses and well-kept buildings.

I do not recall anywhere in the world which generates such a feeling of comfortable opulence as this part of Austria. The houses were in perfect repair, the fields were immaculate and the farmyards were tidy, which in my experience is unusual. English farmyards generally have a few discarded sacks, a few bits of wood and the odd scrap of metal lying about and I had always assumed that this was somehow an inevitable part of farming. It is not so in the farmyards of Austria, which look as if they have been prepared on military lines for inspection by a brigadier.

The principal crop now waiting to be cut was maize, standing about in orderly blocks in the huge unfenced and hedgeless fields. I wondered how they manage without hedges or, indeed, without any detectable boundaries to mark the limits of one man's land from that of another. In the matter of hedges we in England gave our farmers grants to grub them up and make large fields like those in Austria. Then it was found that this led to soil erosion and a shortage of wildlife so they were given more grants to go back and plant fresh hedges all over again. This has always seemed to me to be a most remarkable thing, because governments in England, and probably elsewhere, while they have almost no capacity to leave things as they are, have even less ability to put them back to what they were before. To destroy a lot of ancient hedges in the name of progress is just the sort of thing they would do, but to recognize that this was a mistake and to take steps to undo the damage is not just astonishing, it is possibly unique. I at least can think of no parallel. As far as the Austrians go, from the look of things they don't suffer from soil erosion and don't care about the wildlife.

As well as maize, there were a few blocks of sunflowers, and these I regard as the most expressive of plants. They were now all hanging their heads in that state of gloomy despondency which is always the way with sunflowers in September. It was written all over their faces that they had abandoned the last elements of hope and were merely awaiting the arrival of the executioner in the form of the combine harvester. There were also some potatoes, of a more cheerful aspect, which reminded me of the time that I was pelted with potatoes by an angry German farmer. This was rather a failure from his point of view as I was in a Centurion tank at the time. I was not, for once, lost, but was going about the training area on

Lüneburg Heath on an exercise and to get from where I was to where I was told to go I had to cross this man's potato field. I felt bad about it, but he had chosen to grow potatoes within the training area so he must have known the risks. Rarely, if ever, have I seen a man in such a passion, dancing with fury and screaming with rage as the three tanks that made up my troop churned up his potatoes. Pelting us with spuds was the only way he could relieve his feelings, and as our heads stuck out of the top of our tanks, if he had hit any of us in the eye or on the nose that would have given him some satisfaction. Unfortunately for him his aim was not good enough, so we just trundled on with the rain of potatoes bouncing off the armour plating.

There seemed to be a great absence of living and active Austrian farmers in the part where I now was. There was no noise of tractors, no combine harvesters coming or going, and no visible people, just abundant crops apparently growing by themselves. Had it been Sunday I might have thought they were keeping the Sabbath with strict attention to the twelfth commandment, and doing, as it says in *The Book of Common Prayer*, no manner of work. Whatever the reason it was wonderfully quiet as well as amazingly tidy. At some stage some person had come on the scene and laid out an experimental trial of different types of sugar beet in nine plots. Each variety was in a small bed of its own, and each one carefully labelled. Their names were Flores, Imperial,

Casino, Pingus, Elixier, Baltika, Taifun, Patria and Nancy. Of the nine, Nancy looked the healthiest and Casino the sickliest. For no possible reason these names struck me as being suitable for horses, particularly showjumpers. They seemed to lend themselves to the sort of commentary that you get on television: 'And now, for Austria, the next to go is Wolfgang Vogel on his good mare Baltika – a very nice horse, this – hasn't quite the experience of her stablemate Pingus, but showing great promise and – oh! It's gone!' This means the horse has knocked a fence down, it being the invariable practice of showjumping commentators to tell you what you have just seen for yourself on the screen.

In a little wood in the midst of this farmland I came upon a surprising sign pointing to the Strindberg Museum. Strindberg is not an author I had ever read or, indeed, knew anything about, though I had an idea that he might be one of those melancholy authors like Ibsen, from whom one shrinks because of the gloomy nature of their writing. The only Ibsen play I know anything about is called *Ghosts*. I listened to it through headphones when I was stuck in bed in a public ward of St Thomas's Hospital at the age of fourteen. It was about a young man who went blind from congenital syphilis, greatly to his mother's disappointment, and I did not like it much, so since then I have left Ibsen alone. About Strindberg I am now a little better informed than I was when I saw the museum sign. Having looked him up in *Hutchinson's*

New 20th Century Encyclopaedia, I can tell you that his dates were 1849–1912 and that he was Swedish. Ibsen, of course, was Norwegian, and perhaps that is where the gloom comes from, brought on by the long cold winter nights and drinking too much schnapps. Strindberg was, says the encyclopaedia, 'a strong critic of contemporary Swedish society,' which does not sound the most exciting of topics, and, 'although thrice married a woman-hater and' (as I suspected) 'a deep pessimist.'

The road to the Strindberg Museum turns off from the Donauradweg, and I rode down it for at least half a mile, passing some more immaculate houses and further impeccable farmyards, with no sign of life beyond a whiff of manure from time to time, and nothing whatever to indicate a museum. As I failed to find it, I cannot tell you with any certainty what it contained, but I think the answer includes, rather surprisingly, pictures.

There is a sign saying 'Eizendorf' at the point where you turn off to the museum. If you look up Strindberg Eizendorf on Google (or, in my case, ask someone else to do it as I am incapable of such things) it says 'Did you mean: strindberg eisendorf'. This is a particularly stupid question as if you look up strindberg eisendorf (the computer having unaccountably abandoned capital letters as well as question marks) you get mysterious entries such as 'Tips Perg' or 'Babice u Uherské Hradiště'. If you stick to Strindberg

Eizendorf you get a lot of stuff in German, some of which hints that the museum is not in Eizendorf anyway but in a place called Saxen. If you try 'Strindberg Danube' you will find that in 1893 Strindberg moved to Austria with his new wife, Frida Uhl, and they lived happily by the Danube while he painted pictures for their soon-to-be-born baby. If you apply to something called 'Wikipedia' you will be told that it is not widely known that Strindberg was a painter as well as a writer. Having thus demonstrated that the computer can lead you on a dance all round the subject without getting to the point, I can now save you the trouble by revealing that the museum is indeed in Saxen, is open at weekends from May to October, and has, among other things, pictures. From the map I would guess that the short ride from Eizendorf to Saxen is a pleasant one, in more of the fertile desert through which I had just passed, all of which may be useful information for any Stindberg fan who may chance to read these pages.

The Radweg rejoins the Danube after that most pleasant agricultural excursion and brings you to Grein. You come straight into the middle of things without any of the unattractive outworks that have to be got through at Mauthausen. The centre of town is up a steep hill, which is a wise precaution as the Danube seems to flood pretty frequently. Wherever you go there are marks on the walls to show the levels reached in different flood years.

I felt very well disposed towards Grein once I had got a room, which took a little time, as it was the first place to put up any resistance to the idea of letting me stay there. Three hotels and a *Gasthaus* all claimed to be full and another hotel and *Gasthaus* were locked with no one to answer the bell. However, the Information Office is in the care of a friendly lady so keen to help any traveller who may turn up and so eager to explain the finer points of Grein that she had opened for business at 1.30 p.m., although her office was supposed to be shut till 3 p.m. She solved my accommodation difficulty in a trice with one phone call. She got me a single room at the Goldener Kreuz Hotel just next door to her office, where I had rattled vainly on a locked door, although if I had hunted around a bit more I should have found another door standing open with a man inside and waiting for customers. Having settled that matter she gave me a quantity of invaluable leaflets and told me to enjoy my time in Grein and to come back if she could be of any further help whatever.

I may say that the behaviour of those staying in all those full hotels and *Gasthaüser* was most mysterious as there were plenty of people around during the day but that evening the town was almost entirely deserted. I wandered from one shut eating place to the next, until at last I found one attached to a hotel where a pleasant middle-aged *Hausfrau* was sitting on a chair doing nothing, but evidently in sole charge. She was, I discovered, waitress, cook and cashier all in one, or prepared to be, had there been a need of any such services. I asked if I could occupy a little of her time by eating there, and she said she was only supposed to serve residents, not one of whom was anywhere to be seen. She relented however, and gave me goulash and salad, the goulash tasting as if it had come in a package from Tesco. I wondered very much about all the people who had filled the hotels and *Gasthaüser*. It was, I think, a Wednesday, and I was ready to eat at about 8 p.m. so either they had all gone to bed extraordinarily early, or they had collectively agreed to go somewhere else that evening for some purpose or entertainment, or possibly what the lawyers sometimes call a 'frolic' of their own.

Grein is small and pretty. Everything you want to see except the castle is in the main square of noble, mostly baroque, buildings, with a fountain in the middle. The town hall was built in 1563, says the local guide, and the fountain in 1636. There are cobbled streets and houses from the sixteenth and seventeenth centuries, some with sloping gables, some with ornamental patterns made in plaster on the front. It all speaks of prosperity, which came originally from taking tolls and pilotage fees on the Danube. There used to be a dangerous stretch of rapids after Grein and boats and rafts had to take on pilots to get them safely through the hazards. Then the rocks were blasted away in the nineteenth century, putting the pilots out of work, so I think the present prosperity of

Grein comes from taking money off the multitude of cyclists who pass through.

The theatre at Grein is not to be missed. Indeed, if you set foot in the Information Office, to miss it would be difficult as the lady there insists that you visit it. She is right because it is unlikely that you will see anything quite like it anywhere else. It is small, wooden, painted, ornate and was made by conversion of an old granary in 1790, the work being done by local craftsmen. It is, says the guide, 'the oldest secular theatre in Austria,' which seems to imply that the other theatres were run by clergymen, but secular in this case means, I gathered, that it was the creation of the people of Grein by private initiative, rather than some kind of state or public undertaking. It has been kept most carefully in its original state, with seats for about 140 people. Those in the front three rows are unique in that they can be folded up and locked, the keys being allocated originally to subscribers as a form of season ticket. A professional company performs there in July and August, and local amateurs in the autumn.

They have also carefully preserved the toilet arrangements, in the form of a wooden thunderbox in a cubby hole at the end of one of the rows. This is screened, not very effectively, by curtains, and anyone sitting on it could part the curtains and watch the performance if they so wished. It struck me that this would have delighted the eighteenth-century novelist Tobias Smollett, whose idea of a good joke was a chamberpot emptied over the head of one of his characters. He would have built a whole scene, if not a whole chapter, round a visit to the play and the thunderbox at the theatre of Grein.

Castle Greinburg is high above the town and a little way outside it, approached by a pleasant walk and a bit of a climb. It originates from the fifteenth century and has had many changes of ownership and plenty of adaptations since then. Nothing that I could say about it would do it anything like justice compared to the leaflet which they give you as you go in. The castle, this tells you, 'was built from the brothers Heinrich and Sigmund Prüschenk. They were important moneyspender to emporer Friedrich III. The imposing building is with his generous conception on of the first castles in the german speaking chamber.'

Then, 'the entrance of the castle guides sideway in a gate of the enormal tower. The inner of the castle welcomes the guest with a look in the magnificent court of round arches. The room of the cellular construction is from the late middle age of the building. The fine work of wonder with his faszinating playing of light and shadow was probably built with the saxon master builder Hans Coelin.'

I was, unfortunately, not able to visit the Coburger Celebration Rooms because 'Seeightseeing only with a guided declared tour – not less then 10 persons,' and there were no other persons. This was a pity because, in these rooms, 'the precious equipment is giving an look inside the tensioning career from the House of Saxe-Coburg and Gotha in a europian dynasty. The nobility gender be born die Royal house of Belgium, Portugal, Greatbritain und Bulgaria.'

There is, in more sober language, much to be said for Castle Grein. The Court of Round Arches rises in three tiers of such arches on each side, set with stags' antlers – an impressive sight – and there is a fine grotto decorated with a mosaic effect using stones from the Danube. Anyway, I do not mean to mock the language of the leaflet. To me it shows the go-ahead spirit of Grein. It is the sort of place where they knock up their own theatre out of an old corn store, keep the Information Office open when it is meant to be shut, and when they want to translate something into English, the fact that no one knows the language is not regarded as an obstacle.

There is also much to be said for the Goldener Kreuz, otherwise Golden Cross Hotel. My room, at €46, was quiet and comfortable – a proper room with a chaise longue and an 8-foot mirror in case I wanted either to lounge around or look at myself. It is one of the good things about Austria that they still have single rooms, whereas in many parts of the world, such as London, they only have double rooms and you pay the price of the room regardless of whether there is one or two of you. The huge spread at breakfast next day had all the cold meats and cheeses particularly popular with the Germanic races and the black bread that is particularly popular with me. I supplemented it with a glass of German champagne which I took medicinally having got, at the time, a very slight cold. As a remedy it is to be recommended, as it worked.

The approved way to go on from Grein is to cross the river on the ferry to the right bank. The Donauradweg is marked on the left bank also, but the Information lady had said that this was just a narrow track beside a busy road and that it was much better on the other side. There is a bridge, but that involves cycling back some way towards Mauthausen, and the ferry was the better idea. The ferry is only a little one. It starts at 9 a.m. and to catch it you need to be there in good time. I arrived at 9.15 to find a long queue of about forty people, and as every one of us was equipped with a bicycle each of us took up a great deal more space than normal. The ferry had no special place for cycles, so we and our bikes had all to be squashed in together somehow from bow to stern. There was no room for me on the first ferry and I only just scraped onto the one after that, but it was a quick crossing, and I was soon pedalling along a small and peaceful track on the right bank from which I could see the busy road on the left.

The track widened into a road after a time, but a very quiet one, passing through what seemed to be little holiday villages with little boats for buzzing about the river. The ride was varied, sometimes by the Danube in the open and sometimes by the Danube in woods. The trees were an advantage as they broke the headwind which there was on this morning. There was a bit of industrial grot to be got through at a place called Ybbs, but after that the route reverted to a mixture of Danube, of farmland and a few bits of quiet main road until you come to Melk.

As I was booking out of my hotel in Grein I found an English couple of half my age or less, who were doing what I was doing but meaning to go beyond Vienna to Bratislava and from there to Budapest, all in a fortnight. They were, I think, probably a worthy couple, the sort of people who might well be vegans and wear plastic shoes. They reminded me, in a curious way, of the great Austrian geneticist Gregor Mendel and his work with sweet peas. When I was at school, it was thought that those of us who were studying the classics should not be altogether ignorant of science and so we were given a few lessons in biology. I remember most clearly Mendel's discovery that whether sweet peas are dwarf or tall depends on whether certain chromosomes are dominant or recessive. In the case of this pair of English cyclists, he appeared to be tall and dominant, and she small and recessive. As I was last on and first off the ferry I was the first to set off down the Radweg, but they soon shot past me and out of sight. I started to pedal at 10.20 and at 11.20 precisely, exactly when I wanted it, a coffee place arrived outside Ybbs, with them in it. We had a little more conversation. The young man told me, I thought a trifle smugly, their plan for that day: 'Ybbs is coffee, Melk is lunch, Krems is the night.' The young lady beamed approvingly, and the total distance of 77 kilometres was nothing special in terms of length for a pair of their age, but in these surroundings is a kind of madness. To reduce Melk to a mere lunch stop is obvious lunacy because every guidebook makes it plain that while the Danube has been pretty good up to now, in this region called the Wachau it is about to get even better, starting with Melk. They gobbled up their coffee, I sipped mine slowly, they shot off on their bicycles, I sauntered along on mine, and as I arrived in Melk I saw them leaving.

Melk is a superior sort of place, and I could not see any humble *Gasthof*, at least in the centre of things. I booked into a hotel without too much difficulty once I had, by persistent banging on the bell, roused from somewhere a slightly mad old lady who seemed to rule over everything. She wore a long dress, trailing on the ground and with a lacy top, and she looked rather as if she were dressed for a part in some period play, such as *Charley's Aunt*. This lady looked me over with great suspicion as if she had half a mind to turn me away on the grounds that she did not like what she saw, but somehow I passed muster, and she took me in.

My next step was to eat a huge banana ice cream sundae in blazing sunshine on the edge of the main square, by way of lunch. Melk has the same air of burgeoning prosperity as Grein, but even more so, as it is much bigger. It has the same magnificent houses painted in the same glorious colours, a similar baroque fountain and similar cobbled streets. To explore Melk it is best to begin by finding the Information Office, which is at the far end of the town from the bridge by which you enter from the Danube. The people there will give you a map which starts from their end of town and you can follow it easily. If you try to interpret it from the other end you will find yourself staring respectfully at what you think is the *Rathaus* when actually you are in the market square and not in the town hall square at all. Towering above it all is the immense abbey, which looks as if it could itself house the entire population of Melk if there was any reason for doing so. It was built between 1702 and 1736 and for sheer baroque magnificence I have never seen the equal to it.

It belongs to the Benedictines, but I did not see a Benedictine anywhere when I made my visit, though prayers are said in the church at noon. The Benedictines clearly do everything in tremendous style. In thinking of Melk Abbey you must think big, in terms of Buckingham Palace or Hampton Court. One huge courtyard succeeds another, to be followed by another. Along one side runs the museum, which was packed with tourists. Some parts of it I dodged through quickly as many of the contents seemed to be gold and silver church furniture, if that is the right word for chalices and such things, which have a certain sameness in my eyes. There is though a set of striking paintings of the crucifixion, and I think the artist may have been Paul Troger. After the museum comes an astonishing gold and marble hall with a wonderful painted ceiling, undoubtedly the work of Paul Troger, an artist of whom I had not heard before. There is an equally magnificent library with an equally magnificent ceiling also the work of Troger, who was clearly a great man for ceilings. I counted in the library ten shelves rising upwards, six of folio books, one of quarto, and three of octavo, all running by the yard along the wall and all beautifully bound. It would be a hopeless undertaking for me to try to describe the abbey church. It is a blaze of colour and of gilding, it has fluted pillars and painted walls and ceiling. It has a sumptuous high altar. I will spare you any superlatives on my part and borrow from the Benedictine leaflet, which describes it as, 'a magnificent work of art to the glory of God, among the most beautiful baroque churches in the world.' Amen to that, say I, who thought it was superb.

I then went down a curly, highly decorated staircase where, at the bottom, they have put a mirror like those they sometimes have in the aisles of cathedrals so that you can study the roof without craning your neck. The Melk mirror reflects the whole staircase from bottom to top, going upwards to a great height and curling all the way like the tail of a contented pig. When I reached the shop I found they were selling postcards showing exotic looking black chaps doing things with exotic creatures such as camels, elephants and peacocks. Thinking I had missed the original pictures I went back to the start and prepared to plunge again into the melee of the museum, but the lady at the counter explained that they were not there but in the pavilion. To find this you walk through a huge garden, or perhaps it should be called a pleasure ground, if not a park, because when the Benedictines do a thing they do it on a grand scale and have beautiful lawns, perfect flowerbeds and impressive trees. The pictures I was looking for turned out to be frescoes on the wall of an elegant pavilion, the painter being Johann Bergl who achieved striking *trompe l'œil* effects, such as a peacock painted on what looked like a corner cupboard but is just a flat wall. There are also luscious scenes of dusky maidens with baskets of fruit plus a great menagerie of beasts. At the centre is a raised platform with a sign saying 'Mozart Was Here' and I can think of no better surroundings in which to have heard him perform.

When I checked out of my hotel next morning the money was taken by the same old lady who had checked me in. She was still dressed as if for *Charley's Aunt*, and I had to wait for a time while an American woman gushed at her about how marvellous the breakfast had been. It hadn't particularly, but she succeeded in bringing a smile to the face of the old lady, which is more than I was able to do.

Leaving Melk I went wrong for the first time by cycling down an enticing avenue of trees by the river, which led to a pile of stones with a young man sitting on it doing nothing. He told me I had missed the turning to the Radweg, and I then had to go back and fight my way through a huge crowd of tourists who had been deposited by a riverboat and were making for the town. Once on the right route I came, after a little, to a surprising phenomenon in the shape of a serious hill. You are directed to it by a Radweg sign and find yourself on a main road with no cycle track and a huge hill before you. I felt quite affronted by this, as I had got so used to bowling along on the flat that I had assumed the whole route to Vienna had been, as it were, ironed out. There was no one else going up or down on a bicycle and there were no reassuring signs to say that this was the right way. I think they were rather ashamed of it. It was very hot, so I toiled upwards for quite a time wondering if I had somehow gone wrong until eventually a cyclist with a loaded cycle appeared from the other direction to give me confidence.

I mentioned before that anyone keen on rollerblading might be able to rollerblade from Passau to Vienna if they felt like it, but that there was one difficulty to be got over. I had in mind this hill. I suppose it is possible somehow to get up a long steep hill on rollerblades, possibly by walking sideways, and if so, and if it is possible to shoot down the other side without falling over, then otherwise it is all plain sailing.

Having conquered the climb, I had the satisfaction of a bit of freewheeling down the other side, a unique experience on this trip. After several days of pumping away on the flat, the bicycle in high gear and my legs going like well oiled pistons, it was quite exhilarating to fly along so much faster than usual with nothing to do but sit still. Once back by the river I knew that I must look out for the castle of Aggstein, which was once the stronghold of robber barons who preyed on merchants passing below. It was, I knew, perched up high and I was pedalling away with the river on my left and hills on my right but no sign of any castle, when suddenly it appeared, up on a peak and visible for miles. The pointed end of what was once the chapel stands out with great clarity, as the castle is built on the edge of a sheer drop on the Danube side, so there is nothing to impede the view from below.

The road to the castle was much too steep to ride up so I locked my bicycle to a convenient tree at the bottom and set off on a two-and-a-half-kilometre walk through cool and beautiful beech woods. The castle, once reached, turned out to be the sort of well-preserved ruin that I had expected. Stairs to climb and stunning views along the Danube valley, with wooded hills all round, are what you get at Burg Aggstein. It has towers, a kitchen, a dining room and a chapel all in a state of bare stone, and a most useful cafe. As I was drinking a Coca-Cola out in the courtyard I had my second encounter of the trip with a fellow countryman, or rather, fellow countrywoman, in the shape of a black girl of thirty something. She came up and spoke to me, and we had the following conversation:

She: 'I know your face from somewhere but I cannot think where. Are you an internal auditor?'

I, in some surprise: 'Why do you say that?'

She: 'Because I am an internal auditor, and one internal auditor can usually tell another.'

I: 'No, I am not an internal auditor, but I am a retired local government officer. Perhaps retired local government officers look like internal auditors – or perhaps you audited me when I was still working. We used to be audited by the District Auditor – did you work for him?'

She: 'No, I work for Deloitte.'

I: 'Then it is a mystery.'

There we left it, but I suppose she had a faint recollection of having seen my face on television some years before. Had I chosen to prolong the conversation and given her a hint or two it would have ended like this.

She: 'I know – you are Harry Enfield's father!'

I: 'So I am.'

I should perhaps explain that having somehow stumbled into television I acquired a second-hand existence, not as myself but as the father of my son. He is, for those who have not heard of him, a popular comedian, and so people who recognized me never said 'Hello – you are Edward Enfield,' but always, 'Hello – you're Harry Enfield's father.' As I only got on to television because of his celebrity I had no reason to complain, but it felt odd as if there was no such person as me in my own right but only as Harry's father. I should not be surprised if this idea followed me to the grave, and they put on my tombstone:

Here lies Edward
Father of Harry Enfield
Comedian.

That could possibly puzzle generations yet unborn as it might not be clear which of the two of us was the comedian. It would be better in Latin, which I should anyway prefer:

Hic jacet Edvardus
Henrici Enfield comoedi
Pater benignus

I have added the word *'benignus'*, meaning 'the kindly father' as the Latin seems to demand an extra word for the sake of the rhythm, and anyway I don't see why I shouldn't have a little credit on my own account.

On the way down from Burg Aggstein I met a very fat man who was on the way up. He was perspiring freely and had taken off his shirt. He asked me a question in German which I did not understand, but then he switched to English.

'Am I halfway to the castle yet?' he asked in a desperate manner.

'Yes,' I assured him, 'at least halfway,' though I thought it might be rather less but I was anxious to keep his spirits up. He heaved a sort of doubtful sigh of relief, and then turned manfully to face the rest of the climb.

Having put the hill behind me and done my duty by Burg Aggstein I was now able to enjoy to the full the delights of the Wachau. This is the name given to the stretch of river between Melk and Krems, about 20 miles altogether. The Danube is rather narrower than before, there are little old towns along the bank and there are vineyards all around. I had meant to stay that night at Weissenkirchen on the opposite bank, and came to a ferry with the boat on the other side. There was a couple waiting to cross, so I asked if it was Weissenkirchen that I could see. No, they said, it is Spitz. Well, Spitz looked very pretty, and if I didn't like it when I got there I could always cycle on to Weissenkirchen, so I decided that I would cross. As I waited the male cyclist of the waiting couple gave me some plums which he had picked out of the hedge.

The ferry, when it came, seemed to me to be little short of a miracle. It was operated by one man, who both sold tickets and worked the boat; it was big enough to take cars; it went from side to side with remarkable speed and yet it had no engine. There was a cable stretched up in the air from either bank and the ferry was attached to this cable by another cable and a pulley. It seemed that the captain, if that was his title, had only to put the ferry at an angle to the stream and the force of the current carried it quickly and silently to the other side. To get back to where he started he simply angled it the other way. Of all the truly green, planet-friendly means of transport this must surely be the greenest and the eco-friendliest ever devised. I later described this astonishing device to a friend who is a retired officer of the Royal Engineers and instead of being impressed he was rather dismissive of it. He behaved as if it was something that any competent sapper could rig up with some bits of rope and a pulley, but if it is as easy as that you would think it would be more commonly done.

Spitz, when I arrived by this most agreeable means, was just as attractive as it had looked to be from a distance. It is quite small, and it has the most lovely houses, baroque as ever, and behind it is a great hill covered in vines. It was, by the time I got there, quite late, so my first concern was to find a *Gasthof*, which I did without difficulty, and then to eat an excellent risotto, out of doors and by the river. Being now most definitely in the wine-producing area I asked, almost certainly unnecessarily, for wine *'aus der Gegend'* which means 'from the area'. They would surely have given me local wine anyway but the phrase was provided in *Berlitz German for Travellers* so I thought I may as well air it. The top grapes are, I discovered, Rieslings and Veltliners, and as everyone knows Riesling but I for one had not come across Veltliner, it was Veltliner I asked for. I have since drunk Austrian Veltliner wine in England, and very good it is, but there was something about that first glass taken in the fading sunshine by the Danube at Spitz, and drunk after a good day's cycling and climbing, which lifted it into a class of its own.

Next morning Weissenkirchen arrived almost at once as it is only 3 miles from Spitz. It seemed to be almost another Spitz in its own right, equally pretty, with a fine marketplace and it would not much matter which of these two you stayed at as long as you stayed at one or the other. The reason I took only a cursory view of Weissenkirchen is that the cycling was so wonderful that I did not want to stop, so I took a quick look round and went on.

The ride from Spitz to Durnstein is wholly, utterly, gloriously enjoyable because it is mostly among vines. I think I like cycling among vines more than any other cycling. I have done it in Burgundy where the grapes produce the most expensive vintages in the world, and the thought of all that money hanging on the vine might possibly have given it an added zest, but I was equally happy in the Wachau. For one thing there is something so orderly and tidy about vines, in the way that they stand in long lines all neatly tied in place, as if they were regiments of soldiers on parade and ready for inspection. Some were beside the track, so I could stop and look closely at them, and see the usually green but sometimes red bunches hanging on the main stem, with a spray of foliage above. Some were high in the hills above, on terraces which must have been the product of an almost infinite amount of patient labour, like the rice-growing terraces in the hills of China.

Also, there is such a feeling of antiquity about vines and wine. There is plenty of wine drunk in the *Iliad* and *Odyssey*, and it has been drunk continuously from Homer's time, and no doubt from well before his time, and will presumably go on being drunk as long as civilisation persists. So much has been thought and written about it, so much wine appears in the Bible, in so many novels and in so many poems, and here was the whole process going on, just as it did last year and will again next year as if it meant to continue until the end of time.

When you come to Durnstein, if you did not know that this was the place where Richard I, king of England was imprisoned, and where, according to legend, he was found by the troubadour Blondel, you would know it pretty soon after you got there. The Hotel Richard Löwenherz (Lionheart) stands prominently next to the Gasthof Sanger Blondel (Blondel the Singer) right by the abbey in the centre of things. The story, so far as I can unravel it, is that Richard was more or less kidnapped on his way back to England from the Third Crusade, where he had got within 12 miles of Jerusalem, but failed to capture it from the great Saladin. Among the people whom Richard had antagonized in one way or another were Count Raymond V of Toulouse, Emperor Heinrich VI of Germany and Duke Leopold of Austria. His safest way home, avoiding their territory as far as possible, would be through eastern Germany where his brother-in-law Henry the Lion was at the head of a group opposed to Heinrich VI, but this did involve cutting through Austria. The difficulty was that during the crusade, after the taking of Acre, Duke Leopold had had the temerity to raise the standard of Austria beside that of France and England, claiming an equal share in the victory and of the booty, whereupon Richard's soldiers had torn it down. Austria was therefore hostile territory, but there was no reason for anyone to expect Richard to turn up there and try to sneak through, so it seemed a reasonable risk. He sailed from Corfu, was shipwrecked near Trieste, and then went on with a small party disguised as pilgrims. The word got out and he was caught somewhere near Vienna.

Leopold locked him up in Durnstein and for this he was excommunicated by the Pope, as the Pope claimed to protect crusaders on the way home, but Leopold took not the slightest notice. He later sold Richard to the Emperor Heinrich and his eventual release cost the unfortunate people of England a ransom of 150,000 marks, for which special taxes had to be raised. The latest *Dictionary of National Biography* says he was kept in Durnstein from December 1192 to January 1193; the *Blue Guide* says he was there from December 1192 'until the following March' and Baedeker of 1900 says he was there for fifteen months. Such is the way with guidebooks. They are always positive in what they say and often positively wrong, so my money is on the DNB. Whichever of them has got it right Richard was certainly there, and the people of Durnstein are very keen on the fact.

I climbed up to the site of the castle where he was held. It is signed 'to the Ruins' and a pretty basic ruin it is, with less to see than at Aggstein but without the long climb to get there. I scrambled about what remains of the ramparts, thinking it was something to have trodden where the Lionheart trod before, and enjoying wide views over the town, the river and the glorious vineyards.

There is at Durnstein an Information Office which they keep well hidden, outside the town by a supermarket, and which they only open at noon, and not at all on Sundays. From this I got, with some difficulty, a remarkably trashy leaflet which is mainly given over to plugging hotels and restaurants, and did not mention the abbey, which is what I wanted to know about. The abbey had no guide in English, which was good in a way, as it showed they were not expecting foreign tourists, but it has the disadvantage that I am not now sure that this, which I thought was an abbey, was not actually a church.

There was outside, according to my recollection, a sign which said it was an abbey. I got, somehow, the idea that it was an Augustinian abbey, rather than Benedictine as at Melk. If I was right, the Benedictines had beaten the Augustinians hollow. At Durnstein there is only one courtyard, instead of several; no library; no wiggly staircase; no garden, and while the church is very fine, it has had about one quarter of the gold lavished upon it compared to that at Melk. The more I think of Melk the more I marvel at the fabulous amount of gold the Benedictines must have accumulated and the great amount they must have paid out to goldsmiths to gild almost everything that could be gilded. At Durnstein they worked on a smaller scale, but they had made a very fine walk with a balustrade on a cliff edge above the Danube, so I came away quite content with what they had done at this, as I thought, abbey. Only now, when I have got hold of Baedeker to see if I was right about the Augustinians, is a doubt sown in my mind. It seems that the Augustinians' (I was right about that) 'monastic church', built 1721–1725, is now the parish church. Baedeker describes the gateway and courtyard and church in terms that I recognize, so we are talking about the same building. It is a parish church according to Baedeker and an abbey according to the people of Durnstein, and there I have to leave it.

I should have stayed the night at Durnstein, but didn't, which I regret. It is a place of narrow streets and very old houses but very many tourists. I ought to have applied my principle of staying at the place I want to see, and so put up at the *Gasthof* of Sanger Blondel and enjoyed Durnstein in the peace of the evening. The truth is that the information I had got before I started the trip was much too sketchy, and my plan was therefore inadequate. You who read these pages may profit by my mistakes.

Had I stayed the night at Durnstein I would have got on better at Krems, to which I rode that afternoon in a leisurely manner through more vineyards, meaning to spend the night there.

Krems turned out to be a large place with fine, very large, houses but no rooms. I went up and down, trying this hotel and that *Gasthof*, only to be told that they were all full. At least two had signs outside saying '*Zimmer frei*' which I thought they might have had the decency to take down under the circumstances. One man said he was sorry that he could not help, but the others seemed rather pleased both with the fact that they had no rooms and with themselves in general. They turned me away with an air that suggested I ought to have known better than to have bothered them. There was one hotel owner who, although he had no rooms, made an obliging effort to be helpful and told me to try at a huge building across the square. Following his lead I pealed on the bell and after five minutes a man put his head out of a fourth-floor window and shouted down to know what I wanted. I shouted up that I wanted a room. He shouted down that he hadn't got one, and slammed the window.

Finally I rode to the Information Office which is in an unhelpful place out of town. At least, it is out of the old town, where it is wanted, and in the new town where it isn't. In this sense it is like the office of Durnstein, and it runs on the opposite principle to the office at Grein, being shut when it ought to be open instead of open when meant to be shut. Eventually a girl turned up and unlocked the door. She explained that there was to be a marathon run at Krems that weekend, and today being Friday, the town was full of marathon enthusiasts. She doubted if any room could be got anywhere, and made it plain that she had no inclination to try. I could perhaps have gone back to Durnstein, but for all I knew the marathon might go through the middle of it and the people there might also have contracted marathon fever and filled all the rooms. The only thing to do now was ride on, and while I am sure there is much to be said about

Krems, which is the centre of the wine trade, I am unable to say it, having only passed through.

There was a good deal of looping about through the town (which actually seemed to be two towns, one called Stein and one called Krems, the Stein town being newer and the Krems town older). Then I got back beside the Danube, and by this time, about 4 p.m., it was very lightly raining. Under normal circumstances this would have been quite agreeable, because it was cool, and furthermore there was no one else about and the Radweg was its usual attractive self. There was, however, a possibility that it might come on to rain hard, and I had no idea when, if at all, a *Gasthof* would appear on this stretch of the Danube. After perhaps 8 kilometres there was a sign put up for people like me, saying that if I turned off to the right the road would take me through a number of villages where rooms could be got. I duly turned, plunged through a forest track and came out into apple-growing country with orchards all round. A bluff and rustic apple grower, in the shape of an elderly man with rosy cheeks and a cloth cap, assured me that I would find a village with a *Gasthof* about 1 kilometre further on.

On I went, and came upon a man who was busy building a house with his own hands. I asked if he could tell me where I might get a room and he replied in German which, even to my untutored ear, seemed to be remarkable. His voice went up and down in a most odd way, a kind of melodious chant or almost as if he was doing some sort of music hall turn, an imitation of a Swede, perhaps. Anyway it was perfectly clear that in 300 metrés there was a *Gasthof*, and if that failed, after another 300 metres there was a private house which let rooms.

Sure enough, the *Gasthof* turned up, and feeling pretty confident of success in this remote spot, I wished the owner good evening and asked for a room. I began now to suspect that there is a race of *Gasthof* owners who do not like to clutter up their rooms with guests. *'Wir haben kein Zimmer'* (we have no rooms) was all the answer I got. That indeed was all he said. He did not return my greeting. He did not explain that his rooms were, unfortunately, all under repair and not fit for habitation, which is the sort of thing that happens in Italy, where hotel rooms are frequently *'in restauro'* and out of use. He did not say that he had got rooms but unhappily they were all reserved for marathon runners. All he said was 'we have no rooms'. So I left him and applied, by now fairly despondent, to the house with private rooms. Greatly to my surprise a very friendly lady said I could certainly have a room in the bungalow across the courtyard from her house. She gave me what would have been rather cramped as a double room but was more than adequate as a single one. The bathroom was across the corridor but it was my bathroom, there being two other rooms with two other bathrooms for anyone else who might arrive. The price was €16, with breakfast, or about £12.

That was all satisfactory, but there remained the matter of dinner. I am a great believer in the boycott. I boycott any tradesmen I don't like, and I sometimes boycott whole countries. I boycotted the entire French nation for a time because of the disagreeable way they blockaded our lorry drivers into their ports, owing to some dispute which their farmers were having with their own government and which was nothing to do with us. I would not drink French wine, I tried to avoid French cheese and I certainly would not go to France. These stern measures brought the perfidious Gaul to his senses after a time, and normal relations between us were then restored. I was, however, now most reluctant to give my valuable custom to the disagreeable *Gasthof* man and so, in drizzling rain, I set out on a reconnaissance to find some other place to eat.

I came out of my room, faced resolutely in the opposite direction to the *Gasthof* and walked steadily away. The village was called Thallern. It was an ordinary sort of place, if I may so describe it, with ordinary houses and not a bit like Grein or Spitz. Thallern, I discovered, immediately adjoins another village called Angern. Where Thallern ends, Angern begins, the two village signs being back to back. Angern had an impressive white castle above and a promising *Gasthof* below, with a sign saying '*Weinhof Aufreiter*'. *Weinhof* clearly means a wine house, but *Aufreiter* was more difficult. I supposed it to be the German for an outrider, whatever, in this context, an outrider might be; or else perhaps Herr Aufreiter was the owner. I went in and found the bar full of jolly apple growers relaxing after a hard day in the orchards, so I drank a glass of beer, sized up the elegant dining room, went away and came back at 7.15 for dinner.

The pleasant and helpful waiter put me at the corner of an empty table for four, which was the only available space. He suggested that I have the four course menu of the day, so I did, and it was minestrone soup, salad, fish and apricot dumplings. The fish was pike, and both it and the apricot dumplings were new experiences. They were pretty good, and the whole cost, including tipping the waiter, was about £12, all of which was in its favour. Even so I can only say that the food, taken as a whole, was little more than ordinary, like the houses. It confirmed my impression that Austria is a country not for gourmets but for wine-bibbers, as the *Viertel* of white wine that went with the meal was delicious.

This idea was further confirmed by a couple with their grown-up son who came to fill the three empty places at my table. They asked if I was just there for the wine, which they seemed to think would be perfectly normal. From the look of the place, and the class of the customers, and the quantity and quality of cars outside, I got the impression that this was a place where the smart people came to eat and drink. Possibly, though, they were all refugees from the marathon. The three at my table certainly were, as they too had not been able to find anywhere to stay in Krems, and had rung around until they found this place. As well as being refugees they were also beneficiaries of the marathon as their business was selling sports shirts to runners and cyclists and athletes of one sort of another, and they had come to Krems for this purpose. As my landlady had told me that her three rooms were all booked for the next night because of the overflow from Krems, it is clear that the marathon brings with it a high tide of prosperity, filling all eating, drinking and sleeping places for miles around and creating great opportunities for the sellers of sports shirts.

Next morning I had breakfast with two middle-aged ladies who had been in one of the other rooms. We struggled bravely in German, which was slightly easier than it might have been as they also had cycled from Passau, so we could exchange elementary remarks such as 'beautiful', 'baroque' and 'many people'. On my landlady's advice I did not go back to rejoin the Radweg where I had left it, but went on through Angern on a quiet road which put me back by the Danube a little further on. I passed two more *Gasthäuser* on the way, and there may be a useful point here for any who are inspired to come after me. The authorities who rule the Radweg have this most helpful habit of putting up a sign, from time to time, showing that if you turn off at this point or that point there are places where you can eat or sleep within a reasonable distance. As I really had no plan for the night before, beyond hoping that something would turn up, the sign in this case was invaluable. It is all done with symbols, such as pictures of beds and of knives and forks, so no linguistic skill is needed to interpret them.

The distance from Krems to Tulln, where I planned to spend the next night, is a little over 20 miles. As I had got some way beyond Krems the night before, and as I was in cycling mode, and as there were some pleasant orchards and a minor vineyard or two, and as the sun was shining on the sparkling Danube, and bearing in mind that I had plenty to think about from the day before, I seemed to get to Tulln in no time at all. I realize that Information Offices seem to figure largely in this narrative, according to whether the people were helpful, as at Grein; unhelpful, as at Krems; or in the wrong place, as at both Durnstein and Krems. My favourite of all was the one at Tulln because the young lady there put me into an even better mood than I was before by complimenting me on my excellent German. Apart from *'Grüss Gott'* I had spoken exactly eight words meaning 'Please could you tell me – is there a bank near here?' But it seems that I said this with such elegant fluency that she was struck with admiration. I can only conclude that Berlitz German for travellers is a very beautiful language and that while the locals are doing the equivalent of dropping their aitches or having trouble with their glottal stops, we Berlitz speakers enunciate with a refreshing purity of diction.

The same lady told me, with engaging frankness, that there wasn't much to see at Tulln. The best bit was by the river where there were pleasant gardens and a statue of a Roman emperor. She otherwise recommended the Roman Museum (shut), the Bone House, where they display old bones dug out of cemeteries (no thank you), and the Roman Tower. This I found to be a round stone building that had once been part of some Roman fortifications, though later adapted to become a salt store. When I arrived the door was open and a man in a highly embroidered rabbinical-looking skullcap was standing outside. I said *'Grüss Gott'* without thinking and immediately wondered whether this was a proper greeting for a rabbi, if such he was. He did not seem at all put out, but took me to view the inside. On the first floor there was an empty room with a bar but no barman, nor, indeed, anyone else. There were some beams which the Skullcap man said were very old. On the second floor was a big room with tables laid out in long lines as if for some serious purpose, with pens and paper. Skullcap said there was to be a meeting and as we came out the people for the meeting were arriving. They were all men and they were all in uniform dark grey suits and all had white flat caps on their heads, like bus conductors in a hot country, or old-fashioned ice cream vendors. They were advancing on the Roman Tower in a purposeful manner, and obviously Skullcap was their leader, though leader for what purpose I cannot guess. Perhaps they were freemasons, but if not, they certainly looked like a brotherhood of a rather mysterious nature.

I left them and went to find the Roman emperor, who overlooks the Danube and is mounted on a horse. Horse and emperor are in bronze, on a stone plinth about 10 feet high, and thus well above my head. The horse appears to be champing at the bit, but there is no bit, as the emperor rides without saddle or bridle. He has his hand extended towards the further bank of the Danube, clearly indicating to those on the other side that they are to stay where they are and not to trespass into the territory of Rome. It is an impressive monument on a fine site with, as the Information lady said, a pleasant garden behind.

The inscription on the plinth is this:

Der Römische Kaiser und Herrscher
Marcus Aurelius
Antoninus Pius Augustus
161 N. Chr – 180 N. Chr

I carry just enough German and just enough classical knowledge in my head to be both puzzled and enlightened by this. The word *Herrscher* was new to me, but I supposed it to mean leader or something like that, so that I took the first line to be 'The Roman Emperor and Leader'. In this I was a little adrift, as *Herrscher* actually means 'ruler'. The names

Marcus Aurelius

caused me a moment's doubt. If I go steadily at it I can recite the names and dates of the Roman emperors from Augustus to Commodus. I knew that Marcus Aurelius succeeded Antoninus Pius as emperor and I could not see why both their names were on the plinth. The dates, however are absolutely clear. Antoninus Pius was emperor from AD 138 to 161, and Marcus Aurelius from AD 161 to 180, so obviously the statue was of the latter. I presumed, therefore, (and rightly, as it turns out) that his full name must have been Marcus Aurelius Antoninus Pius, plus the title Augustus, which was always given to Roman emperors. I now know that he was the nephew, adopted son and later son-in-law of Antoninus Pius. My learned friend Dr Peter Jones tells me that he started life as Marcus Annius Verus and accumulated all these other names as part of the adoption process.

Anyway, Marcus Aurelius it was, an emperor best known for his *Meditations*, the personal philosophical diary in which he sets out his thoughts upon life and death and the world and one thing and another. They were, says Matthew Arnold in his essay on the emperor, 'jotted down from day to day, amid the business of the city or the fatigues of the camp, for his own guidance and support, meant for no eye but his own, without the slightest attempt at style.' My mother used to quote Marcus Aurelius as saying, 'If the cucumber you are eating is bitter, quietly take another – do not say, "Why are such things allowed?"'. I cannot vouch for the accuracy of this, but his *Meditations* were translated by the seventeenth-century clergyman Jeremy Collier, who gives one passage as: 'When you find an unwillingness to arise early in the morning, make this short speech to yourself: "I am getting up now to do the business of a man; and am I out of humour for going about that which I was made for, and for the sake of which I was sent into the world? Was I then designed for nothing but to doze and batten beneath the counterpane? I thought action had been the end of your being."' These are both wise sayings, particularly the one about the cucumber. If everyone got out of bed as soon as they woke up I suppose there would be an increase in productivity of one sort and another, which would gratify politicians and economists and people like that, but I think the gain to the world at large would be greater if we all stopped complaining about things that hardly matter, such as bitter cucumbers.

That will give you an idea of his writings, and as for what he might have been doing in Tulln, Matthew Arnold explains, with the elegant clarity that makes him such a pleasure to quote, that, 'the barbarians were pressing on the Roman frontier, and a great part of Marcus Aurelius's nineteen years of reign was passed in campaigning. His absences from Rome were numerous and long. We hear of him in Asia Minor, Syria, Egypt, Greece; but, above all, in the countries on the Danube, where the war with the barbarians was going on – in Austria, Moravia, Hungary. In these countries much of his Journal seems to have been written; parts of it are dated from them, and there, a few weeks before his 59th birthday, he fell sick and died.' A footnote says that he died at Vienna, on 17 March AD 180.

The statue is on the way out of Tulln and having seen it, the garden, and the Roman Tower, I felt I had seen all there was to see in Tulln, and there seemed no reason why I should not go on to Vienna, so I did. The distance is not much more than 20 miles and I quite soon came into the outer suburbs of that city. I was, for a time, riding behind a man in particularly ridiculous clothes. It seems to be the wish of those who make cycling gear also to make the cyclists look as foolish as possible, and they had fitted this man out in a shiny purple top with red and yellow stripes and the words 'Liquidgas Brescia LAT'. Why a man should wish to go about in such a silly garment is a mystery, and partly to avoid looking at his back and partly to gather strength to face the big city, I stopped at a roadside bar for a glass of beer.

Beer in Austria is unpredictable stuff. It sometimes comes in large amounts and sometimes in small; sometimes in a glass and sometimes in a tankard; it is sometimes clear and sometimes cloudy and I never felt that I had much control over any of these factors. I asked now for a small bottle, but the woman in charge said she had no small bottles, so I had a large bottle, and when it came the beer was cloudy. In England I would have objected but there was a boisterous party of five men and a woman at a nearby table, and I could see that they were all drinking cloudy beer, so I assumed that it was the proper stuff, and drank mine. It tasted all right and it set me up for my encounter with the big city, and I think it did rather more than that for the girl of the boisterous party. The rest of them left her and rode ahead while she was finishing a call on her mobile phone. When she set off to join them she went too close to the kerb, caught her pedal on it and fell over sideways with a crash into the road. The others were riding on leaving her sprawling in the gutter, but I shouted and one of them kindly came back and picked her up. She was not hurt, just a bit unsteady owing to the cloudy beer, and did not fall over again, or not until she was out of sight.

I was still riding by the Danube, which now had buildings on either side, and signs saying *'Zentrum'* to indicate the centre. So far as I had a plan, it was to get to the middle of things and see if the Hotel Regina still existed, this being where my wife and I had stayed in 1957. I knew that it was near St Stephen's Cathedral so partly by following *Zentrum* signs and partly by asking for the Stephansdom I got to where I wanted to be and found that the Regina was no more. There were other hotels but the one I applied to was impossibly expensive because, as the man explained, it was inside the Ring.

The Ring is the key to everything in Vienna. It sounds like an opera but it is actually more of a tram track. The trams run round on a wide road going in a circle, and that which is within the Ring is superior and that which is outside is inferior. The cathedral, the opera house, the Spanish Riding School are all within, and as the Ring is only 4 kilometres long, and as Vienna is very large, the bulk of the city is actually beyond the Ring, but most of what you want to see is within it. Or so it seems to a casual visitor like me, though Vienna lovers may protest that there are wonderful parks and museums and churches on the outside.

As all hotels within the Ring seemed to be much too expensive I set off in the direction of the railway station, where they were said to be cheaper. Just before I crossed to the wrong side of the tracks I went into another hotel which looked possible, if only because it was a sort of last chance saloon. If I went any further I should cross the tramlines into Outer Vienna, so I boldly pushed my bicycle up to the desk and asked if they had a room for two nights. As the man was pounding his computer to see if they had a room for two nights, I said, 'I'm probably wasting your time as it will be more than I can afford.'

'In that case I must give you a special price,' says he, pounded the computer some more, and we struck a deal. So I stayed just within the Ring, which is a good idea if you can manage it, as you can then easily walk to most of the bits that matter.

Next morning, at breakfast, I became a serious disappointment to the head waiter. An ordinary waiter asked for my room number and I said 'four-seven-two' or something like that. After a few minutes he came back bringing with him the large, important-looking and fairly ferocious head waiter.

'What is your room number?' he demanded.

'Four-seven-two,' said I.

'There is no room four-seven-two,' said he, in a way which combined both menace and triumph. I felt in my pocket, fished out the little plastic card which operated as a key. 'Four-two-seven,' I said. 'Sorry.'

The head waiter gave a grunt, glared angrily at the card and went reluctantly away, with an air that seemed to say that I had got away with it this time but had better not try it on again. I do believe that he thought he had, at last, caught someone who had come in off the street to cheat him out of a free breakfast. In all his years as a head waiter he had been waiting for this moment when he could take a man such as me by the collar and throw him out of the door, to the admiration of all the other people in the dining room. I felt almost sorry that I had spoiled his big occasion.

I had a busy and enjoyable day in Vienna. The horses at the Spanish Riding School had got the day off, so there was no performance, but there is an excellent film at the museum which shows you exactly what you would see if they were performing. In some ways it shows you more, because the individual high school movements are very well illustrated and explained, in addition to a recording of the whole balletic display. The horses are Lipizzaner stallions, and are so called because they originated from Lipizza in Slovenia. In my travels I have been to Lipizza and ridden a Lipizzaner, but I rode a mare accustomed to put up with semi-skilled tourists and was not allowed onto a stallion from the high school. They do not let people like me onto horses like that, as the stallions will only tolerate the most accomplished of riders, and chuck the other ones off.

The stables at Vienna were also shut, which I was sorry about. I knew what to expect from our visit fifty years before. You see these athletic and dignified animals performing their astonishing routine, and then you go backstage, as it were, and find that they are absolute babies. They come up to the front of their boxes to be stroked and patted, and if you offer one of them a Polo mint the next one starts to bang the door of his box with his hoof to make sure he is not forgotten. They seem to be the gentlest of creatures, and never put their ears back or bare their teeth as some unpleasant horses have a way of doing. Such, at least, is what we found half a century before, when my wife and I visited them, but they may not allow visitors quite the same free access now as they did then.

The horses are white, and so is everyone else in Vienna. This seemed to be the case, as far as I could see, everywhere else in Austria. If you go to London if often seems that the ethnic minorities are in the majority, and in Paris it is just the same. Not so Vienna. Neither Vienna nor Linz, let alone the smaller places, were multi-cultural in the least – in fact they were as mono-cultural as can be. This came as a surprise. I wondered if it was a legacy of the wicked Jorg Haider, but later was told, and now believe, that it is because Austria had no colonies. We had an empire, the French had an empire, and ex-colonial people seem somehow to be drawn to the countries of their former rulers – a phenomenon by which Austria was plainly unaffected.

Vienna is too big for me and I have little to tell you about it that you could not find in any guidebook. I went dutifully to the Stephansdom which seemed dark and crowded so I came out. I wandered about among the tourist crowds, gazing at undeniably fine buildings and unmistakably noble statues, but thinking I would rather be back in the Wachau. Then I was persuaded by a tout in eighteenth-century dress to buy a ticket to a Mozart and Strauss concert given by the Vienna Residence Orchestra, and that was a success.

It took place in a magnificent building called the Palais Averspeg, where, the programme helpfully told us, 'the six-year old W. A. Mozart leapt onto the lap of Empress Maria Teresa.' (Why, I wonder?) It is all, as ever, in the baroque style, with pink and green marbled walls and glistening chandeliers. We sat in a half circle on chairs, a small and respectful audience of about seventy or eighty tourists. The orchestra consisted of four girls in *Alice in Wonderland* dresses, with puffy sleeves and wide sweeping skirts, an invisible pianist and four fellows in white ties. The leader, a young lady violinist, had rather distracting facial expressions. She worked away with her bow and she made great play with her eyebrows, looking now whimsical, now puzzled, now serious, now worried. I was not too sure about discipline in the rear ranks. The male clarinetist seemed to be sharing a private joke with a female oboist, and the flautist had a tickle on his forehead which he scratched with the end of his flute from time to time. I got over that as they played us lovely tourist music, full of tunes such as the overture to the *Marriage of Figaro* and Strauss waltzes. The audience warmed up and became properly enthusiastic. Two jolly dancers appeared, a girl and a young man, and danced what I think may have been called the Tick Tack Polka. The girl performed as a clockwork doll which kept running down and having to be wound up, which made us all laugh. There were also two excellent soloists, one a dark voluptuous woman with big eyes who was a pleasure to look at as well as to listen to.

That was the end of my Danube ride, and I parted from the river with some regrets, or at least doubts. I was now to go back, but the Danube was going on. I had followed the route which the German lady in Greece had written out on a table

Mozart and Strauss

napkin, but I rather wish that she had written 'Bratislava' after Vienna, in which case I should have allowed time to go on to the Hungarian border. If, after Bratislava, she had written 'Budapest' I should have gone on to Budapest, and I like the sound of that city, divided in two by the Danube as it is, and probably not overrun with tourists. The Dominant and Recessive couple from Grein were going to Budapest, and as I never read of a pair of cyclists going mysteriously missing in Hungary, I presume that they managed to get there, and to get home. But then again, if I had got to Budapest, when I looked at the Danube as it went rolling on, should I have been thinking, 'Any man but a coward would plunge boldly into Serbia and Romania, or whatever comes next, and strike out for the Black Sea?' Actually, that sounds too dangerous for an old fellow like me, and I think that it is a temptation I could have resisted. As it was, time was up and I had a plane to catch.

It remained for me to get back to Munich by train. The man at Vienna station refused to sell me a ticket all the way, but insisted that I take a ticket to Strasburg only, and then buy another from Strasburg to Munich. This, he said, would save me €30 and as there was a change of train and a twenty minute wait at Strasburg and as everything ran with exact punctuality, his system worked, but in England I would have regarded twenty minutes as a pretty tight connection. I went from Munich *Hauptbahnhof* to Munich airport on a crowded evening commuter train, getting a good many black looks from the crowded commuters as I had to push my bicycle into the thick of them and stand there holding it upright with one hand and clinging onto a strap with the other. I was to fly out next morning so I checked in my bicycle, myself and all but one of my panniers with the excellent Lufthansa, and then went to the Information Desk for help in finding a hotel.

There I was taken charge of by an Indian lady who spoke, as is the way with Indians, a multitude of languages with astonishing fluency. In my time I have worked in Hong Kong, Japan and Thailand, and in each of these there were Indian merchants conducting their business in Cantonese, Japanese or Thai, while we just carried on in English. Here the Indian lady and I talked English, but I was confident that had I preferred French, German, Japanese or possibly Spanish she would have been equally at ease. There was, she said, a shortage of rooms close to the airport owing to some conference or other, but she knew of a hotel a little way off where they would come and fetch me and bring me back and not charge a lot. She rang them up and chatted in German, rang off and said they would be here in twenty minutes and in twenty minutes they arrived.

I got in a car which set off into the darkness and seemed to go a long way into the wilds before we got to a humble hotel standing alone on a country road. The basic nature of the establishment was reflected in a very basic bedroom, the